Blood on the Badge

Arizona: Land of the lawless

By

Steven E. Farley

authorHOUSE

1663 LIBERTY DRIVE, SUITE 200
BLOOMINGTON, INDIANA 47403
(800) 839-8640
www.authorhouse.com

First published by AuthorHouse 06/28/04

ISBN: 1-4184-2204-5 (e)
ISBN: 1-4184-2206-1 (sc)

Printed in the United States of America
Bloomington, Indiana

This book is printed on acid-free paper.

To Scott, my son in Iraq
and I could search the world,
and never find a better one.

Grateful acknowledgment is made to my wife Ann, Hollis Fletcher, Darrell Lashley and Chris Stramiello for there help and support.

Arizona Turkey Buzzards,

Flying high,

Waiting for you,

To ride by!

Table of Contents

Chapter 1

The early morning sky was bright as the four of them rode into town from the south; they were here to rob the bank of, Sedona, Arizona.

Stan Rhodes, was on his way to the sheriff's office to check for messages, for his father, who is the sheriff of Sedona. Stan watched from up the street as the four rode into town and tied their horses to the hitching-rail in front of the bank. He didn't recognize any of them. They were tall, lean and wore dusty range clothes. They also all wore pistols in low-slung, tied-down holsters. Stan went into the sheriff's office leaving the door open to let some fresh air into the musty office. Stan looked at the clock on the wall of the office as it was striking for the eighth time.

This is when the town opens for business for the day. Stan had always helped out around the sheriff's office, but he was not a deputy, he was only twenty, he did look older for his age. Stan watched from the office window as three of the men went into the bank as one stayed with the horses.

He looked on up the street past the bank and saw very little movement, turned and went to the desk to check for messages.

The dull boom of a shotgun followed the flat crack of a six-gun. Stan jumped-up from the chair, looking out the window and saw the three men come running from the bank with mask over their faces, to their horses. Stan ran to the gun rack on the wall holding several Henry rifles. He snatched one of the rifles, grabbing some cartridges from a drawer under the rack, and loading the henry on the run for the door.

Stan ran for the bank as the four hold-up men, spurring their horses, rode north up the street. The Banker came running out yelling, "They robbed the bank, and shot *me* when, I tried to stop *them!*" What few pedestrians where on the street were now scattering, looking for cover.

The four were now galloping up the street away from the bank. They were at least seventy-five yards up the street leaning low in their saddles.

It was going to be some tough shooting. Stan, dropped to one knee, took a deep breath and settled the sights of the rifle on the back of the one with the saddle-bags, hesitated just a second, then slowly squeezed the trigger, as his father taught him. His target jerked and swayed but stayed in the saddle, but dropping the saddlebags to the ground.

As he shifted the sights over to one of the other hold-up men. The Banker let out a groan and fell into the street, raising a cloud of dust that obscured Stan's vision, as the four dug in their spurs and headed out of town. Stan's father came running up to him with a gun in hand, asking Stan if he was all right. "Sure, I'm fine, wounded one of them, he dropped his saddle-bags with the bank's money."

Stan, breathing deeply and wishing that his heart would quit beating so fast, he had never aimed at anything except targets and wild game. There was something very different about shooting at a man. Sheriff Dell Rhodes came back toward the bank with the saddlebags full of the bank's money, and looking down at the banker lying in the street. "Doc, the Sheriff asked, is there any thing you can do for *him*?" Doc Stone, looked up at him and shook his head, "He's dead Dell."

Doc Stone stood up, snapping his bag shut, and ordered several of the bystanders to take the banker's body over to the Undertakers. Bill Shaw was the towns' only banker! Doc, looked at Dell, "I will go and see his *wife!*" The sheriff, turned and looked at Stan, "I want to talk to you over at the office." Stan swallowed. He had a feeling his father was going to do most of the talking.

Dell shut the door of the sheriff's office and went to his desk, sinking into his chair behind it. Stan replaced the henry back in the wall rack, then waited to see what his Pa had to say. "What in blue blazes did *you* think *you* were doing?"

"You could've gotten killed out there with those men!"

"They held up the bank and shot Bill," Stan replied. "I figured it was my job to stop them, *me* being the closest one and all." "Catching robbers is my job, not yours. You ain't an official deputy, and you know it." His father sounded angry, but his tone abruptly softened as he went on, "Darn it, boy, I don't want to see you hurt. What would your Ma say if I let you get killed Fighting outlaws?"

Stan was silent. He held himself tightly, waiting for his father to finish. "Well heck," Dell sighed. He let a grin seat over his face. "You're old enough to know when you're taking a chance. Once you took a hand, you did a darn good job. That must have been one fine shot." Both of them knew what he was talking about.

In a voice that was little more than a whisper, Stan said, "When *it* was happening, all I was thinking about was stopping them and keeping them from hurting any one."

"I know. I wish I could tell you it gets easier in life, but it doesn't. There are times out there when a man has to fight to defend himself or other people. Son, You're going to make one fine Lawman."

The sheriff got up from his chair, "Guess I'd better go send a wire and see if we can find the U.S. Marshal, they're in his jurisdiction, now!"

Marshal Glenn Fuller had been a lawman longer than he could remember, before coming to the Arizona Territory he had been a sergeant with the Texas Rangers in south Texas, chasing renegades and rumrunners. He had been over at Elgin checking on some missing horses when he got the message that the bank at Sedona had been robbed and the banker' had been killed.

The Marshal was only a day's ride from Sedona, so the bank robbery had priority over horses that had been missing three days before he arrived. The rain had wiped out all sign's of tracks and it was unclear if they had been stolen or they took off running during the lightning storm.

As, the marshal rode into Sedona, he rode slowly to the Sheriff's office looking the town over, seeing the closed sign in the window of the bank. As he was pulling up in front of the sheriff's office, when the door opened and the sheriff stepped out to greet him.

"Howdy Marshal, glad to see you, we received your telegram that you were on your way!" "Glad to see you too Dell!" Dell had worked for the marshal as his deputy for over five years until he had tired of the long horseback trips and wanted to spend more time with the family. "How much of a head start do they have on me?"

"They have almost two days on you Glenn, one of them took a bullet from a henry, so they won't be traveling very fast." The marshal looked at Dell. "Who shot him?" The sheriff looked down at the ground and back at the marshal. "Stan, Stan hit him from a distance of seventy-five yard's." As the two were looking at each other Stan stepped out from the Sheriff's office as the two turned to look at him.

Dell looked at his son and back to the marshal saying, "He's going to make some fine lawman, Glenn." Marshal Fuller looked at the sheriff and nodded his head. "I would like for you to send Stan to me when I catch these killer's, I'll need some one to help identify these men if need be!" Stan looked at Glenn. "This is fine with me marshal, it's time for him to get out and see some of this big country!"

Marshal Fuller took his gloves off and reached into his vest pocket and pulled out a silver object and handed it to Stan. He took the object and turned it over, it was a Deputy U. S. Marshal's badge.

"I have two other deputy's but they're off chasing outlaw's over at Green Valley, Stan you are now a Deputy United States Marshal."

The marshal looked at the two of them and saw father and son grinning at each other. "Well if you two come with me over to the telegraph office I'll wire my office and tell them all about you Stan. The marshal told the two lawmen that he thought the bank robbers turned south when they were fare enough out of town, doubled back and headed for the Mexican boarder, should pick up their trail south of here." The blacksmith brought the marshal a fresh horse and the supplies that he asked for in the telegraph to the sheriff.

Stan walked over to the marshal as he was getting on his fresh mount, "Sure you wouldn't want me to go with you."

The Marshal looked down at Stan, "No son, I'll send for you, if I need you."

Stan watched as the marshal rode out of town. He also notices something else about the marshal when he took off his gloves both of his hands had rheumatism in the finger joints just as his Grandfather had!

Marshal Fuller was going to retire at the end of the month and he knew that his hands were not working the way they should be. In this line of work you need every thing working! Only if one of his other deputies had been close by to help him. He didn't want to take Stan with him, a boy still green in this line of work and besides he needed Stan in town just in case they came back.

The next day out of Sedona the marshal came across their trail heading south toward Chino Wells. He knew that they would have to stop for provisions and medicine if the wounded man was still alive.

Chapter 2

You could tell the horse was a mare, and that was about all. Roan, bay or chestnut, whatever her color, it was well hidden under the caked dust. Her rider was little better off. His hat, his bedraggled mustache and his bushy eyebrows took on the same slate-gray color from the dust. You had to get mighty close to make out the dull, shapeless thing on his shirt for what it was-a U. S. Marshal's badge.

He'd been a long time in the saddle, and felt it. The mare dragged her hooves, pluming dust behind here, and he didn't have the heart to quirt more speed out of her, even though it meant that many more hours, or days, before he caught up to his quarry.

He'd stopped thinking what he would do when he met up with them. They were four, he knew, and one man was a poor match for four younger, armed, desperate men. Even unsuccessful bank robbers could be successful killers. But the marshal had something they didn't have: a badge. It was old, scarred, a worthless bit of pot metal. It had pushed him into more danger and brought him out of more danger than he liked to remember. He wasn't a man given to poetic flights, but unuttered in his brain was a tribute to his badge: a shield and a buckler and more than a match for four lawless guns.

The four were watching him right now from the sawtooth rimrock above, watching the plume of dust the marshal left as a token of his passing. And it spooked them.

The four were three and a half, really. Larry Farley, the youngest, lay grimacing in pain on the ground. In his beardless face you could detect a growing resemblance to the stronger planes of the thin-lipped man who bent over him and gently dabbed at a raw gunshot hole in his side with a filthy bandanna. The wounded boy jerked. 'Watch it, Greg!" "Sorry, kid." Greg Farley moved the bandanna with more care around the lips of the wound to clear it off the black oozing blood. The two others glared grimly into the valley. Ben Miller, tough, driving, with a cruel, cynical mouth, disfigured by the knife scar that slashed to the jaw, glanced across at Greg Farley and saw he was occupied. Carefully, avoiding noise, he drew a Winchester from his saddle boot. Gorman watched him and watched Farley, nervously wondering which way to jump. A sharp look from Miller settled his indecision. Frank Gorman, older beaten down by life, was always happier when somebody told him what to do. Miller rested the Winchester in a notch of rock. Greg Farley, without turning, spoke quietly. "Put it up, Miller."

Miller snapped around at the sound of the other man's voice. But he couldn't muster the extra touch of nerve it took to run counter to Farley's tone of quiet authority. He slammed the rifle down angrily. "We gonna let him follow us to doomsday?" "He ain't about to catch up with us," Greg said. "I say get rid of him!" " And I say there'll be no killing!" Gorman squirmed. "He itches me. He sure itches me." Ben grunted. "Me too." Greg laid a hand on his brother's arm. "Take it easy, Larry." Larry pushed the hand away fretfully.

"What's the matter? Afraid of a little blood when it ain't your brother's blood? That's all right, ain't it?" Greg didn't answer, but went back to dressing Larry's wound.

Gorman hunkered against a rock and took out a harmonica. He tapped it wistfully, blew dust out of it, and brought it to his unshaven lips. Miller growled. "Stow that thing!"

"Aw, shucks, he won't hear it from here!" Miller said viciously, "You put it in your mouth an' I'll ram it down your throat!" "All right, all right!" Gorman shook his fist at the valley. "That's another count I got against you, you stump-suckin' Johnny Law! Man can't even have a little music with you in the same county!" He looked at the mouth harp regretfully, then stowed it in his pocket. Greg rose. "We better be moving on." When he unfolded to his full height, he was taller than you'd have thought. Flat of stomach, deceptively slow in his rangy movements, you wouldn't have put him down as possessing great physical strength. But without apparent effort he got an arm under the boy's shoulder and another under his knees and lifted him to his saddle like a child. The pain of getting settled brought a grunt out of Larry, and Greg frowned. Larry managed a meek grin. "I'll hang on, big brother. Don't worry." The sawtooth had given way to the low rolling hills. The four still clung instinctively to the higher ground, although in that country there wasn't much choice between one spot and another. They huddled against a rock in the dark, in a half-circle, as though drawing warmth against the whining, chill wind from a nonexistent fire. Gorman grumbled, "Crazy country.

9

Gets so hot in the daytime, and cold enough to freeze off a Billy goat's whiskers at night. You'd think things would even up a little."

Nobody answered him. Miller turned to look with hate at a pinpoint of light in the distance. The pinpoint was a campfire, and only one man for a hundred miles around could be sitting by that fire, soaking up the warmth they were denied. Greg turned to Gorman. "How far to that town you were telling us about?"

"Chino Wells. Twenty, maybe twenty five miles." Greg poked at the remains of their cold meal. "We got to provision up there." "If we're to keep goin'." "Wasn't for *him*, we wouldn't have to keep goin'." Miller said, jerking a thumb toward the pinpoint of light. Gorman grunted. "Wasn't for *him*, we'd have a fire." They fell silent, each in his own way dreaming of warmth. Gorman spat on the ground. "Elk steak." "Eh?"

"I said elk steak. An' biscuits. Sure would go good right now." Miller turned his back on the old man. "You darn fool." "I remember an elk steak . . .it was in Patagonia. . ."

His lips slavered with the image his mind brought up. Greg said, "Shut up, Gorman."

Gorman shrugged, and jerked his chin toward the distant marshal. "How long you reckon he figures to dog us like this?" Larry said without turning, "Till he gets what's coming to him . . . a slug in the belly!"

"Take it easy, kid. Rest while you can," Greg said. Larry said grimly, "I'll hold out. He's the one ain't lettin' me rest. You shoulda let Miller take him." "I told you before . . . no killing." Miller looked his contempt. "You gettin soft' or something, Farley?"

"We got along fine without it so far, I ain't about to change over now." "There's worse." Larry said. Greg turned to him. "Such as . . .?"

"*Not* killing a man that can put your neck in a rope." Greg thought it over. "Funny."

"What's funny?" "You and me. We' been together all our lives. Everything you know you got from me. How could we get so far apart on this?"

"Maybe I'm beginin' to learn things my self . . .without you. The kid's got to grow up sometime." "I don't object to growin' up," Greg said. "It's the *way* you're growing that bothers me." Larry turned away from him and settled down in the sheepskin, trying to sleep. Unseen by his brother, the boy's face flushed with an old, long-pent-up resentment.

From where he lay, he could see that distant pinpoint of light and his resentment switched to the fire and to the man drawing the warmth that was denied to him. The blasted marshal was mocking them. He wouldn't get away with it. Greg wasn't God.

Larry gave the others a half-hour, so the weariness of the saddle could conquer the discomfort of the cold ground. When he could distinguish the still forms, the even breathing of the three, he struggled to one elbow. Fighting the burning pain in his side, Larry carefully threw off the blanket. Nobody stirred. Slowly he worked his way upright. It was agony to keep from dragging his feet across the gravel, but he managed. The cold, smooth butt of the Winchester felt good and right in his hand, as he snaked it out of the saddle boot. A horse whinnied, and Frank Gorman turned over on the ground. Larry froze, waiting for silence again. Then he turned and disappeared into the brush, limping painfully.

They heard the sound of the shot, reverberating lazily through the still night. Greg Farley sprang to instant wakefulness. Before Gorman and Miller wiped the sleep out of their eyes, Greg's quick eye had noted the crumpled blanket, the empty saddle boot. He turned and saw the distant campfire, a cherry glow now, winks once as someone moved in front of it. Before the others were well on their feet, he was on his horse, making for the fire. He found Larry warming himself by the fire. Larry jerked a thumb. "Move him over, Greg, an' pull up." He shivered with pleasure. "God, it feels good!" Greg stared at him, and then at the still form sprawled in the dust, washed by the flickering light. The black stain spread from his middle shirt button to the badge on his chest. The bullet went through the body of the marshal. He didn't turn as Gorman and Miller clattered up and dismounted. "Get out your mouth harp, Frank. A little music would go good, an' you don't have to worry about nobody hearin', except us. "Larry saw Greg's blank, dismayed look and grinned, "Don't worry, big brother. I wasn't in any danger. A Winchester'll out range a six-gun any day. You know that."

He saw he wasn't making any impression on Greg's granite jaw; his own face went hard. He held open the fleece-lined leather jacket he wore for Greg's inspection. "Look what he had on, the dirty son! Sheepskin! He was warm in this while we was freezin' in cotton!"

'It's a dead man's coat," Greg said, trying to keep the tremble out of his voice. Larry laughed, an ugly laugh. "Well, he won't be needin it no more, That's a sure thing!"

"Take it off," Greg ordered him. Larry stared at his brother. "You crazy or somethin'?"

"Larry . . ." Greg couldn't trust himself to say more. "Aw, let the kid go," Gorman put in plaintively. "It's only a coat." "Sure," Larry said. "Come on up, Greg, an' get some of this fire." Greg made no move toward the fire. He watched, unable to take his eyes off the spreading stain that crawled and spread until it touched the silver badge, on the Lawman's breast pocket. Then, as if satisfied it had accomplished some symbolic goal, it rested.

They came on the town suddenly, too suddenly for comfort. It seemed to slap them in the face as they topped the rise. This was what they'd been beating saddle leather for since the disastrous affair at Sedona. Now that it was within reach, they stopped by unanimous, unspoken consent and just looked. Gorman spoke up first. "That's it-Chino Wells." Miller slapped his reins. "It ain't doin' us no good standin' here lookin'. Let's go."

Gorman shook his head. "Not me. They know me there." "Well, that's just fine! You afraid?" Just the same, Miller reined up. Gorman bridled. "I ain't afraid of nothin'."

"Think they heard about Sedona? I don't see no telegraph wires." "They got the telegram all right," Gorman assured him. "Not that they need it. Way we been travelin', a slewfoot jenny coulda got there ahead of us." Greg opened his canteen and handed it to Larry. "Maybe we ought to give'er a miss," Miller hazarded. Gorman grunted. "Fifty miles of chaparral to the next food an' water." "Larry ain't travelin' no fifty miles," Greg said flatly."Wasn't for him, we wouldn't be in this fix!" Miller shouted out.

"Lay off him, Miller." Greg's voice was low and dangerous. "Well, said Gorman, "We can't *all* go into town, an' that's a fact." "Greg said, "I'll go."

"Well, no use everybody stickin' their neck out. One man's got a better chance." Gorman's relief was obvious. Greg helped Larry painfully get off his horse and sat him gently down in the shade. He straightened up and held out his hand. "Takes money to buy grub. Fork over." Gorman and Miller exchanged glances, dug into their Levis and came up with a small showing of coins and bills. Greg hefted the meager take. "Fine poke for a bunch of bank robbers." "May be better if we bust in the back door of the grocery tonight," Gorman offered hopefully. Greg withered him with a look. "When I take chances, it'll be for something bigger than a side of bacon." He swung aboard his horse. "I'll be back along about sundown. Take care of Larry."

Miller, watching, him ride down the slope, took out the makings, looked at the crumbs of tobacco left in the Durham sack and threw it petulantly on the ground.

"Not enough for one lousy smoke." He said to nobody in particular.

"Not one lousy stinkin' smoke!"

"Maybe he'll bring some makin's" suggested Gorman hopefully.

Chapter 3

It was a town like dozens of other towns that Greg Farley had known and passed through, uncurious, uncared for, uncaring. For these people in the streets, loafing on the canopied boardwalks outside the store fronts, moving about their business inside the barbershop, the blacksmith's the saddlery, it was home: a place with friends and fires, a place, maybe, to pass their whole life in without caring or wondering or needing to know what was over the mountain.

For a drifter, a town was something else again. A town was a bed, a bath, a drink, a woman. Not too many women while he'd been bringing up brother Larry. Right now it was a menace, a place to get in and get out of quickly with the food to stoke the fires to get to-where? Greg turned of his mind from thinking to keep from answering that one, because there was no answer. He passed the Chino Wells Bank. His practiced eye pulled away to rest warily on the Sheriff's Office, with the barred jail windows visible around the corner to the rear. It was close to the bank-too close. The telegraph office was across the street Chino Wells, Arizona over the doorway.

He dismounted in front of the general store and had started for the door when the commotion pulled his head around. The hulking brute in the middle of the street was raging drunk, weaving as he faced a lean cowpoke, while bystanders looked on with varying degrees of amusement. The fight was in the insult stage. Greg spared a second to get the picture. Then he went into the store. What happened to the cowpoke and the drunk meant only one thing to him, and that was good. It meant a chance to get his grub and get out while the townsfolk were looking elsewhere.

The breeze carried the unintelligible snarling voices into the store as Greg translated his spare hoard of cash into beans, side meat and flour. When he stowed the grub on his saddle, the insults were still flying.

"Jus' you watch what you're doing', you crummy sheep-dip cayuse. I'll take you apart!"

"Who you callin' sheep-dip, Moody? I got a good notion . . ." Greg didn't bother to turn his head. He couldn't have cared less. "Look out! He's got a knife!" There was real urgency this time, and the scattering of the crowd brought Greg's head around.

"All right. You come one step closer . . . " It was the drunk talking, the spring-blade knife flashing in his fist. Darn fool, Greg thought. The cowpoke drew iron, but the drunk called Moody was surprisingly quick for a big man. He flipped the knife with an underhand motion as the other man's gun muzzle blazed fire. The slug went wild; the cowpoke gripped his gun arm in pain, dropped the six-shooter and sank to his knees.

Greg went back to securing his provisions. The fight was over. But the sound of another voice froze him. "Pop! You hurt him!" A boy of ten or eleven ran out under the elbows of the crowd and tried vainly to hold the big drunk

16

and keep him from following up his advantage over the fallen man.

Moody got hold of the kid's arm and shook him like a fly-whisk. He said thickly, "I'll hurt you too, you skunkin little pest. Lemme at him . . ."

"No! Pop, don't do it! You'll get in trouble again!" Greg stopped cinching his saddlebag and started toward the two. Vainly the boy was trying to pull his father back; heels dug in the dirt, puny muscles straining. The kid got spunk, Greg thought. Men on the boardwalk shouting with laughter.

The drunk, disconcerted by the boy's dragging weight, turned and glowered down at him. "I'll fix you!" He gripped the boy with one hand and readied the other for a blow that could have shattered the boy's jaw. But at the top of the upswing, his wrist was caught in a manacle of steel. "Let the kid alone," Greg said quietly. Moody whirled. "You keep out of this!" "I said to let the kid alone. "The boy stopped struggling in his father's grasp. "Watch out, mister! Pop's a fury when he's likkered up! He'll . . .'

The drunk squeezed the boy's arm, and the youngster cried out in pain. Almost simultaneously, Greg loosed his cocked fist. He felt Moody's sandpaper stubble scrape skin off his knuckles. The boy tore free as the big drunk started a roundhouse at Greg.

Greg moved one step back, and then two steps forward to give drive to a fist that sank deep into Moody's belly. The whole town was watching now. The ones who'd run away at the first glint of the knife were back. The barber, with poised razor, struggled with his half-lathered customer

17

for space in his narrow window. The swinging doors of the saloons were held open by knots of men with shot glasses in their hands; and even the bank suspended operations for the spectacle. A girl elbowed her way between the men and pressed her face against the glass. The final tribute to her dark-eyed beauty was the fact that the prim shirtwaist, the alpaca sleeve dusters and the raven hair gathered into a bun too old for her years could not dim it. She took in the situation at a glance: the big drunk on the ground, fighting for his lost breath; Greg standing over him, easy and relaxed, but with the warning of forked lightning in his hip-shot stance; and behind Greg the boy, wary and scared, rubbing his hurt arm.

The girl's dark eyes flashed disgustedly at the men about her, who gaped and made no move to end the fight; pursing lips that were never made for pursing, she pushed back out of sight, to reappear a moment later. Fighting her way through the second knot of men who blocked the door to the street. Moody had fallen close to the knife half-buried in the dust of the street. His hand snaked out with a swiftness unexpected in such a big man, and with a flip of powerful legs he was back on his feet.

"Pop!" the boy wailed. Then, "Watch out, mister; Pop's death with that knife!"

Greg Farley had already seen a sample of Moody's knife work and didn't need the warning. Legs apart, he tensed ready to spring in any direction, his hand still inches away from the holstered gun at his side. Moody lunged at him; Greg moved to the right, and the blade caught his left sleeve. Blood began to stain the linsey shirt immediately. But it was blood traded for knowledge. On Moody's next lunge, Greg's own right hand snaked out and caught the thick wrist. This was the sight the girl came upon as she pushed to the front of the ring of spectators. The two combatants were locked as one, straining against one another with sweat and trembling sinews; and despite it all, the point of the knife was coming ever closer to Greg's eyes.

The girl looked on, fists clenched. "Stop it! Why don't you stop it?" she screamed at the fascinated men about her.

"Now, then, Miss Jessica." One patronizing male voice was all the attention they spared her; for the rest, they were living the struggle vicariously. Calling on unsuspected reserves, Greg lunged with the desperation of imminent death and forced the blade away from his eyes.

Twisting powerful shoulders, he hung onto the other man's wrist and bent it past the point of human endurance. The knife clattered to the ground. Moody pulled away and came at Greg with a bull roar. Greg sidestepped, brought up an oak-hard fist that stopped the big man cold, then chopped clenched hands on the back of the big man's neck.

Moody went down in his tracks. The boy scurried in and dropped to his knees beside his still father, sobbing, "Pop! Pop!" Jessica gathered the boy in her arms. "Pop ain't really bad, only when he's like this." Jessica comforted him. "There' there, Gary."

The onlookers had recovered their courage now; they gathered close. A heavy-set, well-dressed man of fifty elbowed to the center. "Miss Jessica, you all right?"

"I'm all right, Mr. Barker," the girl assured him. She caught sight Greg's bleeding arm.

19

"You're cut!" The portly man said, "Young man, I want to shake your hand. That was as fine an exhibition of pure courage as I've ever had the privilege of observing."

"Never could stand sill and see a kid mauled around," Greg said gruffly. Moody opening his eyes' strained forward to get to Greg. Two husky men held him back.

"Come, on, Bill!" one of them said. Gary rushed to them. "Don't jail Pop! Please!"

"It's all right, Gary," the girl said gently. She turned to the portly man. "Mr. Barker, let's get this man to the bank. Somebody call Dr. Brown." "Of course, of course. Please come, sir." Greg cursed himself silently. What had happened to his idea about slipping in and out of town unnoticed? "It's nothing." "Nonsense! Miss Jessica, you help him!"

The touch of her hand on his arm, feather-soft and warm, drove all idea of Self-recrimination' from his mind. He allowed her to lead him, weak as a day-old lamb.

The doctor was an earnest, straightforward young man, who tried to overcome his lack of years with a small beard. He worked on Greg while Barker, the banker, carried on a conversation from his rolltop desk. "You mustn't judge Chino Wells by this outbreak, sir.

Oh, Miss Jessica, there's a customer." Jessica detached herself reluctantly from the trio and went to the wicket.

Greg's eyes followed her graceful movements. He was called back by Barker's insistent voice. "You may have noticed that our citizens seldom carry sidearms. And speaking of sidearms, my dear sir, I can't commend you too highly for your own restraint." Greg caught Dr. Brown's eye. He, too, was watching the girl. "Just a drunk," Greg said. Barker wagged a finger. "A drunk who'd already knifed a man. Faced with a situation like that, not many men would have chosen to settle the matter with their fists." He indicated the six-gun at Greg's side.

Greg said, "Didn't seem like it was worth taking a chance on killing a man." "But you'll find, if you stay here-and I do hope you will, Mr.-?" Greg hesitated, a split-second. "Farley," he supplied. The name meant nothing here' could bring him no harm. "Mr. Farley," repeated the banker. "I'm happy to know you. Figure to stay in Chino a spell?" "I don't think so, Mr. Barker . . ."

"Pity, pity. The town could use more like you-peaceful-minded men. We get plenty of the other kind." Greg only half heard. His eyes were on Jessica again. She was cleaning out the surplus cash from her drawer.

He watched her carry two fistfuls of bills to the iron safe by the bank wall of the room. She passed Greg; their eyes met; she smiled.

A sudden twinge caused by the bandage the doctor was binding around his arm called Greg's eyes back. Dr. Brown had been watching the exchange; he frowned. The doctor was in love with the girl, Greg realized. Dr. Brown expertly tied the bandage. "There. That ought to take care of it, Mr. Farley." Greg rolled down his sleeve and stood up.

"Wait just a moment, Mr. Farley." Jessica caught the sleeve. "Let me mend this." "Oh, that's not necessary, miss!" But he let her ply the needle, while he looked down on her hair. He towered over her. She was not tall, he realized; it was just that she carried her self so proudly that she gave that impression. Jessica bit off the thread. "There! Not a very good job I'm afraid." Greg said gravely, "It's fine.

21

I'm much obliged to you, Miss Jessica." She rewarded him with a smile. "And my thanks to you, Doctor." He reached into his pocket. "Afraid I don't have much to pay you." Doc. Brown said evenly, eye to eye, "That's all right, Mr. Farley. You did the town a favor. The town is glad to return it. Just speak kindly of us on your *travels*." He stressed the last word slightly. Greg regarded him gravely. "Sure. I'll do that. Thanks again." He touched his hat to Jessica, nodded to Barker and went out the door. Jessica stood looking after him. Doc. Brown ventured, "Jessica." She didn't turn. "Yes, Jim?" "I was wondering if I could ride out to call this evening?" Jessica's eyes sparkled mischievously. "Yes, of course, Jim. We're always glad to see you." Barker came over to them, leading a portly man in a square derby and a flowered waistcoat, whose carefully cultivated mutton-chops and thick gold watch chain he spoke a personage of significance. "That young fellow," Barker asked, "Where did he go?" Jessica was transparently innocent.

"Young man?" "You know who I mean. Mr. Farley." "Why, Mr. Barker, how should I know?" Doc. Brown looked at her reprovingly. "He went into the saloon across the street." Barker said, "Oh, Dr. Brown, come inside a moment, will you? Colonel Bailey and I would like to consult you about something. Jessica, dear, keep an eye on the Satin Slipper, will you, and let me know when this Farley fellow comes out. Don't let him get away." Jessica lowered her eyes demurely. "I won't, Mr. Barker." Doc. Brown looked at her as he followed Barker and Bailey to the inner office. Jessica took up a station at the window, were she could keep the Satin Slipper in view.

There were eyes on Greg in the bar. He could feel their pressure, even as he looked down at his drink. He'd come in, not because he needed the whiskey, but because it would look strange for a man-especially a man who'd attracted so much attention-to leave town without stopping for a drink. He'd be all right; Greg told himself if the old drifter next to him would only keep his mouth shut.

The drifter slapped Greg on the shoulder. "Yes sirree! Jest walk' right up to that loco coot, an' wham! Take the knife right outa his hand." He buttonholed anyone who would listen, making the most of his nearness to a celebrity. "Swear to Jehoshaphat, I never seen nothin' to match it!"

Greg didn't want to shut the old man up, but he wished he'd get over reliving the morning's excitement. There were' a couple in the group at the bar of whom Greg instinctively was wary-a couple of hard-looking cases if he'd ever seen any. He knew his instinct was right when the bigger and uglier of the two chimed in, speaking to no one in particular.

"Pretty brave feller, takin' on a blind drunk." The old drifter was quick to defend his prize. "Drunk, sure . . . With a knife! A plenty dangerous catamount!"

The hardcase seemed to reconsider. "Maybe you're right. Brave man like that deserves a drink." He moved closer. "What'll you have, brave feller?"

"I've still got this," Greg said mildly. "Brave man needs *two* drinks. Bartender, bring the brave man another drink!" The hangers-on sensed trouble. They backed off, ready to duck or run. Greg turned his back to the bar and leaned on his elbows. He spoke quietly and steadily. "Anything special on your mind, mister?"

The bartender set a bottle in front of them and backed away fast. The hardcase reached over and started to pour a drink into Greg's half-filled glass. Greg very casually moved the glass, and the whiskey spilled on the bar.

The hardcase turned ugly. "Why, you Son-of . . . "

He went for his gun. Greg's gun snaked out of his holster and the bullet cut into the gun arm of the hardcase. He fell to the floor in pain. The crowd in the bar gathered around the hardcase, as Greg put his gun back in its holster and walked toward the batwing doors. A delegation was waiting there. Barker, Colonel (Mayor) Bailey and Doc. Brown had evidently been watching the scene with fascination. Barker turned to the Colonel. "Well, Mr. Mayor, does that settle any doubts in you mind?" Bailey said, "It certainly does." Doc said, "I still say no. We don't know anything about this man."

"Doctor, we're not doing him any favors." Barker said. "It's a dirty, dangerous, thankless job we're offering, but it's got to be done. You know anybody in town we can ask? Well do you?" Doc Brown was silent. Greg reached the three and stopped.

"Mr. Farley, would you be good enough to permit us a word with you?" Greg looked them over, hesitated. "We can talk in my office, Barker said. Greg waved them ahead, then followed them out to the street. The old drifter sidled up to the man nursing his arm.

"Fast, ain't he, Morgan?" The man called Morgan lashed out and knocked the drifter, grunting, against the bar. The old man went down, crashing heavily into the dust and beer puddles on the rough plank floor.

Morgan's scowl dared anyone else to speak up. No one accepted the invitation. The patrons gave him plenty of room as he went to the door, viciously kicking the prone drifter in the groin as he stepped over him.

Chapter 4

The second conference in the bank was clearly of serious importance. Jessica, at the teller's window and not been invited, mad no bones about cocking an ear to listen when her duties permitted. "Mr. Farley," Bailey said, "I was not present at the disturbance which you handled so ably this morning, but I witnessed enough just now to realize that what I heard was not exaggerated." Jessica came forward, "Mr. Barker, The Wells Fargo stage is here,"

"Ah! Excuse me a moment, gentleman." Barker hurried around the rail. Bending an inch, Greg could see the stage outside. Bailey was talking, but Greg only half heard. He strained to catch snatches of talk outside.

"Always glad to see you fellows . . ."

"Marshal Fuller took after 'em. He'll get 'em . . ." Bailey tapped him on the arm.

"I asked, sir, if you are free to entertain a little proposition we've been thinking of offering you." Greg turned back to him reluctantly. "Proposition?"

"I'll come to the point-although that's not easy for a politician to do!" He laughed heartily at his own joke. "By and large, this is a peaceful town, but of course now and then a crisis does come up. As you should well know, Mr. Farley!

For some time now, the more responsible citizens of Chino Wells have felt the protection offered by the Federal Marshal is not sufficient. Marshal Fuller is a good man, but he has to cover too much ground. As *you* can see, when we needed him, he was off south somewhere."

The others failed to notice Greg's sudden slight tension. "Yes," Bailey went on, "mighty lucky for us, you happened around just when you did, Mr. Farley." He stopped short and looked at Greg piercingly. "Chino Wells needs full-time law enforcement, and we're ready to pay for it."

Jessica cut through the fog of verbiage. "Mayor Bailey is offering you the job of Sheriff of Chino Wells, Arizona, Mr. Farley," she informed Greg. "That's about it," The Mayor admitted. "We've talked it over, Mr. Farley. We're convinced you're just the man for the job, if you'll take it. Temporary appointment, of course, pending approval of the town council, but I assure you that's just a matter of form."

He waited to see the effect of his words, then added persuasively, We need a man like you, Mr. Farley: tough, but on the side of the angels, so to speak." Greg was genuinely stunned. "I don't get it," he said. "There must be plenty of fellows . . ."

The Mayor shock is head. Chino Wells is small, Mr. Farley. There are not as many as you'd think. Not the kind we'd trust." "Trust?" "That's right, Mr. Farley. Twice in the last hour you've shown us you're the kind of man we need." Greg's steady gray eyes' were an impregnable mask. "You don't know anything about me."

"We've seen enough, and your own reticence just now does you credit," the Mayor said with conviction. He took a sheriff's badge from his pocket and placed it on the desk. The sight of the shiny bit of metal exerted a queer, almost hypnotic fascination on Greg. He was conscious of quiet expectation; they were waiting for his decision.

He tore his eyes from the badge to look at Jessica. She was patiently eager to hear him accept, this girl who hadn't set eyes on him an hour before . . .

There'd been other girls for Greg, of course, other women. Something about him attracted them. But with this girl it was somehow different. Her wide dark eyes were completely honest, unabashedly candid, yet without the slightest hint of cheap flirtation. Greg turned from her and looked over at Doc. Brown.

This was a different story, a different story entirely. "How about you, Doc?" Greg asked.

"You in favor of this?" Doc wasn't a liar, whatever else he might be. "I'll give you a little pain killer to take if that arm starts bothering you." He handed Greg the little bottle with the air of paying off an obligation, paying in full, irrevocably. Greg took it, nodded his thanks and, to escape Doc's hostile gaze, turned casually to where the clerk and the driver, under the watchful shotgun of the guard, sweated to transport a heavy, brass-round chest from the vault to the door. Barker was hurrying back to them. "You asked him?" Mayor Bailey nodded. Greg stood up. You'll accept, Mr. Farley?" Barker was anxious. 'No, gentleman. But thank you for asking me." He nodded farewell and headed for the door. Doc shrugged. 'Well, I told you. He turned you down cold.'

"After the way you answered him, what did you expect?" Jessica flared at him. Doc said coldly, "He asked me. I wasn't about to lie . . .to a drifter." Greg sensed the eyes boring into his back as he went out the door. The clerk strained with the effort of hoisting the chest aboard the stage. Voices drifted to Greg's ears. "Anyway, this bank won't be worth robbing for the next few days. 'Course, we're expecting Mr. Brice . . . close to forty thousand dollars . . ."

"Too much cash for one man to lug around . . . all the way from Abilene!" The driver kicked the chest and shook his head disapprovingly. The shotgun guard put in his two bits worth. "Well, he won't trust us . . . got to take his chances." The voices faded as Greg continued down the boardwalk. Small, fast heels drummed on the walk behind him. "Mr. Farley!" He turned to face Jessica, who was running toward him. Behind her, and separately, Doc Brown came, also walking fast. She was about to speak when the Doctor grasped her arm. "Jessica . . ." His tone held a shocked warning. Greg watched, impassive. She bridled at interference, he noted. He liked a woman with a mind of her own, a mind that could be changed by the right man, naturally. None of the three noted a tired rider wheeling in fast toward the bank. He reined up and slid off leather, then went inside at a run. Jessica made no attempt to hide her displeasure. 'What do you want, Jim?" Doc said, "I'd like to talk to you, alone." Greg touched his hat. "If you'll excuse me . . ."

"No. Stay, please, Mr. Farley." The girl's tone was imperious. She looked at Doc Brown questioningly, challengingly. Doc said, "I just don't think you ought to try to persuade Mr. Farley to change his mind." "Mr. Farley doesn't impress me as likely to be persuaded to do anything he doesn't want to do," Jessica countered sharply. Mayor Bailey, Barker and the dusty rider came out of the bank, saw the three talking in the shade, and hurried over. Barker called out, "Mr. Farley! Jessica!" Mayor Bailey panted, "Marshal Fuller . . . he was found killed!"

"No!" "Over past Squaw Butte range, " the rider volunteered. Barker said, "More than that . . . the bank at Sedona was held up by four masked men . . ." The Driver said, "Fuller was trailing 'em when they got him." He spat out his contempt. "In the back."

Barker spoke earnestly to Greg. "You see this puts a different face on matters here, Mr. Farley. Now we're entirely without law protection, and those bandits are at large. Won't you reconsider your decision?" He spoke quickly, forestalling Greg's possible objection.

"If it's a question of money, the bank is willing to put up funds to double the salary originally offered by Mayor Bailey."

He was holding out the badge. Greg looked over their faces. All, with the exception of Doc Brown, were hoping anxiously for his acceptance. Down the side street, he could see Gary Moody talking to his father through the bars of the jail.

There was a clatter of hooves and wheels, and a shout from the driver and the shotgun guard as the stage thundered by them. Their remembered talk rang in his ears. Jessica had taken the badge from Barker. She held it out to Greg like a chalice, like a gift, in her cupped hands.

The forty thousand, Greg told himself harshly. That was why he took the badge, touching the girl's soft hand with his rough, grimy fingers. That was why he pinned it on his shirt and became the sheriff of Chino Wells, Arizona.

That was what he told himself, over and over. And deep down inside, he could never be really sure.

Chapter 5

Larry lay on the ground next to the campfire, shivering even in the fleece-lined windbreaker. He'd tried to sleep, but the pain of his wound wouldn't let him. He cursed the snoring Miller and Gorman, cursed the brother who'd deserted him, cursed the world and his luck, dam' the luck. If he ever got out of this unholy mess, things were sure as in-hell were going to be different. Just how, he was too sore and too miserable to try to figure out. But let him get on his feet again; just let him get back on his feet!

The faint whinny of a horse tensed his body, shooting the pain up his side and forcing him to bite down on the gasp that rose in his throat. He reached over, nudged Gorman and cautioned him to silence. Gorman woke Miller and put his finger to his lips. The horse could be heard plainly now, coming closer. The roan mare picked delicately between the rolling boulders and flood-cut potholes. Greg, peering ahead, made out the campfire through the brush. The faint light glinted on his chest. Acting on impulse, he took the badge off his shirt and buried it in the pocket of his jeans.

Three guns faced him as he came into the clearing. He grinned. 'That a way to greet a man?" Gorman was on his feet, eager. "Them the groceries?" Greg, dismounted, knocked the older man's hand away from the bag. He kneeled down by Larry. "How you feelin', kid?" Larry screwed his mouth into a bitter curve. 'Lot you care. Where the devil you been?" Greg paid no attention to the outburst. He brought out the little bottle. I got some pain killer here." He helped Larry swallow, then reached into the bag. 'Here, take a chew of this. Remembered you like it." Larry's anger evaporated at the sight of a long sausage. He grinned. "Well, are the rest of us gonna get a look at them vittles or not?"

Miller grunted heavily. "You shore took your time." Greg pushed the bag toward them. "I got delayed. Interestin' town." He proceeded to bed Larry down more comfortably, then offered him his canteen. "Only interest I got is to see it disappear over the next rise; Gorman said, his mouth full. "They got a bank?" Miller asked. Gorman said, 'They sure have! Big one!" Greg's eyes narrowed. "They had a bank at Sedona, too," he said casually.

"Remember? We didn't come out of it so good."

"That was just dirty bad luck," Larry said.

"We'll really take 'em this time!" Greg raised his brows.

"We? Where do you think you're going'?" Larry chewed on the brick-hard sausage.

"I'll be fit in no time."

"You'll stay put, kid, till you heal up." Greg punched the boy's jaw playfully.

"What about us?" Miller asked belligerently.

"Larry can't travel. You know that."

"He's your brother. That don't mean the rest of us got to stay here an' be sittin ducks."

"Nobody's keeping you," said Greg mildly. Gorman held up his hands. "Now wait a minute. We, can't go high-tailin' off by ourselves, you know that. Not without no grub, no money; an' the Lord knows how long it'll be till we find our next stake." Miller was not to be downed.

"You could case that bank, Farley, an' the three of us could take it." Greg didn't answer, and Gorman asked curiously, "What's the matter, Greg? Something wrong?" Miller's voice turned nasty. "Looks like he don't want to take that bank. What is it, Farley? Scruples? Or just plain yellow?" Greg's fists tightened and he took a step in Miller's direction. Miller's foot dropped back, and his hand went to his gun butt.

It was Gorman, the peacemaker, who took over, rambling amiably as if nothing had happened. "They got a bank all right. Handles three times as much as that crib over to Sedona. What d'ye say, Greg? We need a stake." Greg turned away without answering and hunkered down by Larry. The boy said, "They're getting' spooked, waitin' around like this."

"I don't like it," Greg said in a low tone. "They might get a notion to take it out on you. I can't be with you all the time." Larry was still cocky, in spite of his weakness.

"Don't worry about me! I can take care of myself!" He reached for his gun and winced with pain.

"You couldn't fight off a jackrabbit, and you know it," Greg said. " 'Course, if you told 'em you'd case that bank' that'd hold 'em." Larry looked at Greg sidewise. Greg compressed his lips and kept silent. "You got some reason not to do it?" Larry asked.

"No, of course not," Greg said shortly. He turned and saw Gorman, casually whittling at a branch, straining his ears to listen. "I'll talk to you later." Larry threw back the windbreaker as the fire worked into his skin. Greg's quick eyes caught something he had not seen before: a pair of initials burned into the leather where the buttons had hidden them before. Two initials: G. F. for Glenn Fuller.

A dead man's jacket', A murdered man's jacket. And the murderer wore it with out a twinge of concern. And the murderer was his brother. Greg turned to the fire and warmed his hands at the glowing chaparral twigs.

Once again he saw the sprawled figure of the marshal on the sand, beside another fire, saw the spreading red-black stain on the U. S. Marshal's badge. The jacket would have a bullet hole in the back, too, Greg thought. But it would not be big enough to let the cold through.

Not big enough to admit the chill of conscience, Greg closed his eyes and tried to force the image out of his mind. He didn't have much luck. Greg was up before first light; with out waking the others, he rode back to town.

Chapter 6

A husky man in a leather apron plied a broom over the rough plank floor of the dingy sheriff's office. He looked up as Greg entered with Mayor Bailey. "Marshal Fuller used the place when he was in town, so you will probably find out." Bailey caught sight of the sweeper. "Oh, hello, Fred. Shake hands with our new Sheriff, Mr. Jordan." The Man shifted the broom and wiped his hands on his apron. 'Please t' meet you!"

"This is Ray Tuttle, who owns the livery stable down the street," Mayor Bailey explained. "Heard you was comin'," Tuttle said. "Tryin' to get the place tidied up a bit for you." Greg shook his hand. "Howdy, Mr. Tuttle." Tuttle said, "Terrible about the Marshal, isn't it?" "Ray's been droppin' in, kinda takin' care of the place between times . . . feedin' the prisoners, when we'e got 'em," Bailey said. "Guess I'm more at home with mules, Mr. Mayor." Bailey moved the papers on the desk, raising sun flecks of dust.

"Afraid I can't help you much with all this, Farley. You just do what you can about it.

As I told you, it's a peaceful town. Mainly, just seeing a badge around will hold down most of the riffraff." His eye caught one of the papers; he picked it up and read it. "Here's a report on the bank robbery at Sedona. Hmmm." Greg turned to the cell to conceal his expression. Moody peered out at him. "Judge should be out this way some time next week. He'll hold trial then." Mayor Bailey replaced the report. "What about the men who killed the Marshal?" Tuttle asked.

"That's outside Mr. Farley's jurisdiction. 'Course, if they should happen to come this way . . . But we hope they won't." "Amen to that!" Tuttle gave a final lick to the floor, then put up the broom. "Well, any time I can help you, just yell, Sheriff!" Greg nodded. "Thanks I'll do that." "The same goes for me, Sheriff, or for that matter, anyone else in town. Lots of luck."

Bailey held out his hand, and Greg took it. "By the way, you'll be wanting a place to stay. I suggest The Bailey House." He smiled. "Special rate for public employees." Greg did not return the smile. "Thanks, Mayor he said soberly. 'I'll be over." Greg sat before the desk after Bailey left, with a weariness he hadn't suspected till now. It had been a strain, all right. He looked over the papers on the desk aimlessly, unable to make much out of them and caring less. Without moving, he took in the dinghy office-the rifles and shotguns in their rack, the worn, dust-covered notices and bounty papers on the unpainted pine wall. He opened drawers in the desk, and found boxes of cartridges, a tin of snuff and a big iron ring of keys.

He took the keys to the gun rack and found the one that opened the restraining bar.

Only on turning was he conscious that he was not alone. The bleary, hollow-eyed gaze of Moody followed his every movement from behind the bars. Now he spoke timidly.

"Mister." Greg turned to him. "Yes?" "You're the feller slugged me yesterday, ain't you?" "That's right." "I want you to know I'm right sorry."

Moody's tone was sincerely humble. "Don't know what got into me, to take off that way." Greg grunted. "I know what got into you." Moody nodded sadly. "Sure . . . the bottle. Never could hold it." "You ought to lay off it, then." "I will! So help me, I will!" Moody cried earnestly. Greg reserved comment.

He knew Moody's type-wild when drunk, sorry when sober-until the next smell of whiskey undermined his puny resolve and rendered him helpless in its sodden fumes.

Moody hesitated. 'The other feller . . . the one I cut . . . how's he doin'?"

"Doc says he'll recover." "Thank God! I been praying' for him all night." Moody shook his head. "Dunno what coulda got into me!"

"He was pushin' you around!" Greg turned at the new, fierce voice. Gary Moody, tousle-headed, straddle-legged, uncompromising, tried his best to fill the doorframe with his small body. "Pop don't take no pushin' around! Do you, Pop?"

"Now, Gary . . ." Moody began. "He started it!" Greg had to admire the kid. "The judge will take that into account, Gary." Gary's eyes widened. "Judge?"

"That's right. Be here next week, Mayor Bailey tells me." "You gonna keep Pop in jail till then?" "Reckon so, son." "Even if he makes bail?" Greg tried not to smile. "Where'd you learn about bail?" Moody spoke shamefacedly from the cell. "Guess I give him plenty of opportunity, Mr. Farley."

"Well?" demanded Gary truculently. Greg said, "I don't have any authority on that, but I'll find out." He moved up to Gary with a shooing motion of the hand. "Now you better run on home. This ain't any place for a kid.' Gary stood his ground. "You know what, Mr. Farley?" "What is it?" Gary said seriously, "I thank you're gonna make a good sheriff."

He turned on his heel and disappeared. Moody said ruefully, "An' he oughta know."

"Seems like a good kid," Said Greg. "Yeah. Little wild sometimes, but I guess I don't help him none that way." "What about his mother?" "Dead," said Moody. "Dead two year now." Greg kept silent. Moody shook his head. "Things'd been different if . . ."

"He stopped, looking toward the door. Greg followed his gaze. Morgan, the hardcase who'd tried to draw on him in the saloon the day before, came in the door, followed by a swarthy man with an evil, snag-toothed grin. "What do you want?" Greg asked coldly. Morgan turned to his companion, ignoring Greg completely. "What d'ye know, Hobbs? The brave man's *sheriff* now!" Greg rose. "You got anything on your mind, spill it."

Bill Moody peered from his bars, a worried look in his bleary eyes. "Now take it easy! We don't want to tangle with the *sheriff*!" Morgan backed up in mock fright. "Do we, Hobbs?" Hobbs was highly amused. "No siree!" he exclaimed. Morgan jerked a thumb toward the cell. "What you figure to do with him, Sheriff?" "What's that to you?"

"Man he cut was from our spread." "So?" "So we figure he's our beef, not yours. You let him go, we'll take him off your hands." Greg shook his head. "No dice," he said shortly.

"Now, Sheriff, be reasonable! Judge comes to town, gives him three months, six months . . ." Moody called out, "Yeah! Lemme out, Mr. Farley! I'll take care of them!"

"Shut up," Greg said, without taking his eyes from Morgan. Morgan was the dangerous one. Hobbs took a step toward Moody. "We'll give you the same chance you gave our friend. Greg said, "You're wasting your breath, boys. Now get out." His quiet confidence caused them to back toward the door. Morgan tried again. "What's the use feedin' the big ox for three months when we . . ." "Out," Greg said, without raising his voice. "Aw, come on, Morgan; we ain't getting' nowhere around here." Without Hobbs backing, any thought of ganging up on Greg went out of Morgan's mind.

"Maybe some other time, oh, Mister Sheriff?" "Sure," Greg said easily. "Some other time." He opened the door for them. "Any time at all," he added significantly. He watched them mount up and take off down the street toward the north, then turn back into the office. Moody said, Couple of mean hombres. Nothing' to do but roister around till their boss gets back from Abilene." Greg's brows contracted slightly at the word Abilene.

"You know," Moody went on in a worried voice, "My shack's right next to the Lazy S, an' them skunks know it. Just like 'em to tear apart the place for the heck of it." He shook his head concernedly. "Not much they can damage, but . . ." "But what?" Greg asked him.

"Gary's out there." "Alone?" Moody nodded. "That's just it." Greg carefully kept his voice even. "You said the Lazy *S*?" "Biggest in these parts. Old man Aaron

41

Brice drove more'n twelve hundred head this time." Greg considered "When's he due back." "Can't be too soon for me. He's the only one can control them bushwhackers when they go on the prod. I sure don't like it, Mr. Farley." Dan got up and reached for his hat. 'Maybe I'll keep an eye on Gary.'

"Moody's incredulity was plain on his face and in his tone. "You will, Mr. Farley? You can't miss my place. Just past the Lazy S gate." "I'll find it." He stopped momentarily at the door as Bill Moody's grateful voice followed him. "God bless you, Mr. Farley!"

As he loosed the roan from the worn hitching post, a man and woman passed on the boardwalk. "Morning', Sheriff," the man said cordially. The woman smiled at him. It took Greg a moment to realize the greeting was for him. He touched his hat quickly.

"Mornin'. Mornin', ma'am." Other towns' folks greeted him as he rode down the street toward the end of the false-fronted buildings. Strange how quickly the touch of awkwardness disappeared from his replies. It was kind of easy, getting used to this "sheriff" business. But it was more than that, he knew. Hearing the respect in their voices was a experience for him.

Greg tried to remember when a man, much less a woman, had looked on him the way these people did. He couldn't recall. His only respect had been commanded with the aid of a S & W .44 thumb-buster single-action that slapped against his side. The false-fronts fell away to open, rolling country, a valley cupped in a sawtooth ring.

As he rode, pictures kept coming back. The orphanage that him and his brother had suffered in and the brutal farmer that they bound him out to when he turned twelve and was able to work, letting Larry come with him when he threw a tantrum that nearly tore down the place. The weight of the slop-filled buckets on the end of pipe stem arms, the ache of a small back caused by the stubborn sacks of grain, and the solid, satisfying thwack of the axe handle against the man's shins when he slapped little Larry around.

The two of them took off in the night, and the farmer didn't bother to go after them.

The meals of stolen apples and the fitful sleep under trees and haystacks during those growing-up years. The first gun we ever had, Larry was the one who had stolen it. After that it was easy. With a gun, a boy was a man. And if you didn't object to using it, men jumped, and handed over whatever you wanted. That was what Larry had learned-and what Greg had never been able to stomach. And it ended with two dead men and one of them a lawman lying in the dirt, with 'blood on his badge'.

Steven E. Farley

Chapter 7

A neat, freshly painted white fence gave way to an arch in the hollow, a well-made job that spelled money. "Lazy *S* Ranch," it said over the arch. Greg nosed his mount to the gate, lifted the rawhide thong, and replaced it after he'd gone through.

It was a long way from the gate to the house. This was a lot of property to be fenced. The barns were painted, too, and the low, vine-covered house was a beauty to behold in that land of drab clapboard. The front door was opened to his knock by a, wizened old Chinese, who bobbed and grinned and didn't understand a word Greg said.

"Is Mr. Aaron Brice home?" "*Yessee!*" Greg hesitated. This didn't jibe with Bill Moody's story. But it was too late to backtrack now. "My name's Farley. Could I see Mr. Brice?" A cheerful bob'. "*Yessee.* Sure. *Yessee.*" A woman's voice, coming from the house, cut through the meaningless chatter. "Wong, who's there?" She was at the door before she could have expected an answer: ample, friendly, easy going. Her eyes went to the badge on Greg's shirt. "Oh, good morning. You're the new sheriff. I heard about your appointment." The words rushed out. "Congratulations. We sure needed a man like you. Don't mind Wong. He doesn't understand a word you say." "*Yessee!*" Wong bobbed happily. "Yes'm I'd like to speak to Mr. Brice, if it's not too much trouble." "Oh, did you know? Mr. Brice is in Abilene, selling the stock." That was better. Greg permitted himself a noncommittal "oh?" "I'm Mrs. Brice. Is there any way I can help you? Won't you come in, have a cup' of coffee?" She didn't wait for Greg's demurrer. "Wong makes good coffee.*"* *'Yessee!*" Wong agreed. "Well, thank you kindly, ma'am," Greg said. He knocked the dirt out of his heels and followed her inside to the spotless kitchen. "Sit down, sit down!" She bustled to the cupboard and set out coffee cups and biscuits, her tongue never stopping for an instant.

"Lord knows a body gets few enough chances to talk to somebody, outside of these ranch hands that can't but two words together fit for a lady to hear. I tell you, Mr. Farley, isn't it?" Greg nodded and again tried to speak and was cut short. "Mr. Farley, I was real pleased to hear that Chino Wells got law and order again. And I can see just by looking at you you're going to make a good sheriff."

"Thank you, ma'am. This *is* good coffee." "Hear that, Wong? The sheriff likes your coffee." Wong grinned from ear to ear and all but wagged his tail. "I was wondering, just when do you expect Mr. Brice back?" Greg was carefully casual. "Well, now, I couldn't rightly say," she replied. "You see, he keeps it kind of quiet, what with carrying all that money. Wouldn't do for the wrong ears to be listening before he could get it into the bank." "No, ma'am, it wouldn't," Greg agreed, his face a mask. "I worry about Aaron, I really do." "I reckon he can take care of himself." She clucked, shaking her head. "Time and again I've told him to let the Wells Fargo Company bring it-but he swears that Archie and

Jake are safer than any Wells Fargo shotgun guard that ever lived."

"Archie and Jake?" "Yes, They'd die for him, I do believe. Matter of fact, just two years ago the three of them *was* held up . . .had a running gun battle. Archie's horse was shot out from under him and Jake took two bullets in the side, but do you think he'd let Aaron stop to help him? No, siree! Just said, 'You hang onto that money and get!' An' wounded as he was, he killed two of the rascals, and chased the other until he fainted from loss of blood!"

Greg made a mental note. "Sound like good men." "Oh, they are, more coffee? Heavens sakes, it's stone cold! I'll just heat it up." She was up and at the stove. "I fret myself plumb sick every time Aaron goes on the drive, even though he . . ." She stopped short; Greg felt she was on the verge of telling him something important. "Yes'm?" he said.

"Well, he insists it'll never happen again. Got it all fixed up, he says, but that don't keep me from frettin'. That's a woman's life, my mother used to tell me. Always something to worry about. And it's the gospel truth! If it ain't the little ones, it's the big ones turn your hair gray! There, now, this is better. Hold up your cup, Mr. Farley."

Whatever she'd been about to say, it was lost now "Gracious! Here I am rattling on, and haven't even given you a chance to tell me what you came for." Greg looked at her and said. "It can wait till Mr. Brice gets back. Just a little matter of a couple of your men acting up in town."

"That would be Rex Morgan and that Darrell Hobbs! I told Aaron he should get rid of them! I do hope they haven't caused you any trouble, Mr. Farley." "No, ma'am, none to speak of. I figured Mr. Brice could herd 'em back in line easy enough. 'Course, I didn't know he was away."

"Well, don't give them another thought, Sheriff. I'll treat 'em to a tongue-lashing they won't forget." "I wouldn't want you to mix with 'em, ma'am. They're pretty rough customers." She laughed shortly. "Don't worry about me! I can handle them!" Greg wiped his mouth with the checked napkin and rose to his feet. "That'll be just fine, Mrs. Brice.

I kind of hate to be throwin' my weight around before my boots are dusty on the job."

"And that does you credit, Mr. Farley," she said with conviction. "But if any of our men get out of line, you just step on 'em. Mr. Brice will back you to the hilt, you've got my word on that!" "Thanks, ma'am. I hope it won't be necessary. And thanks for the coffee." "Not at all. Glad to see you any time when you're out this way." She went with him to the door, then stopped. "Oh, I just happened to think . . . are you going back to town, Sheriff?" "Yes, directly." "Would you mind doing a tiny favor for me?" "If I can."

Aaron asked me to pay this before he left, but what with one thing and another, do you know I never have gotten around to it? You know Brown's Feed Store?" She was holding out bills. Greg said, 'Yes'm, I've seen it." Poor Mr. Brown has been so patient! Four' thousand and twenty dollars. You're sure I'm not putting you out, Mr. Farley."

Greg looked at the greenbacks. "Not at all, ma'am. Glad to help." "Thank you so much, Mr. Farley. And don't forget, the latch is always open out here!" The door closed. Greg stood on the stoop for a moment, staring at the bills in his hand. Here it was again, that new feeling. Somebody trusted him; trusted Greg Farley. It was an odd feeling, an oddly good feeling. He stuffed the bills into his vest pocket and walked slowly to his horse.

He didn't head straight back to town, but rode to the top of the rise, where the valley spread below him circled around to the sawtooths. He stood for a long time, looking out to the east, toward Abilene. He turned finally and dug spurs into the roan's flanks. But before he got twenty feet, a rope snaked out of the air to settle across his chest.

The tightening loop jerked him off to the ground. He was on his feet in an instant, the wind half knocked out of him, his hand fighting the loop to get to his holster, before he looked up to see Gorman pulling the other end of the rope. "You dam fool!" Angrily Greg flung the loop over his head as Gorman gave him slack. "You could've killed me! What's the big idea?" "Maybe you better tell *us*, Sheriff!" Miller appeared from the cover of a rock. "Go to blazes!" Greg snapped. "Now, now," soothed Gorman, "Set awhile with your old pals. Remember we knew you before you was sheriff." Greg whipped around and grabbed a double handful of Miller's shirt. "Larry! What did you do with Larry!" Miller looked over Greg's shoulder. Gorman was advancing, his barrel-gripped gun held high. The butt crashed down on Greg's head.

He waken' to the throb of pain and to shimmering figures standing over him. "All right, you dirty rat, tell me why I shouldn't let you have it right now?" Miller snarled down at him. Greg painfully worked himself to a sitting position before he could trust himself to reply. It took an effort to keep calm. This was no time to say the wrong thing.

"Because you'd be killing your chances, that's why." He had them hooked. He could see that right off. The immediate danger had subsided. "Chances?" Gorman queried. Greg felt the lump on his head, all matted blood and hair. "Water," he said. Miller grabbed him the way he had grabbed Miller only minutes before and yanked him to his feet. Greg tensed against the stabbing pain in his head.

"All right, Sheriff. You started something. Now talk." Greg deliberately brushed Miller's hand off and got the canteen himself. He dabbed water on the wound gingerly. Keep them hanging, longer the better. Gorman, as usual, broke first. His voice was a whine. "Come on, Greg, what you got up your sleeve?"

Greg' looked them over deliberately. "How'd you like to make it into Mexico with a full poke? Thousands, Thousands apiece." Quick greed took over Miller's ugly face, to be wiped away by even quicker suspicion. "Stallin' won't help you," he snarled. He cocked the rifle, but Gorman pushed the barrel aside.

"Wait a minute, Ben. Let's hear him out." Greg wiped the dust from the shirt." All right. I wasn't goin' to let you in on it. I figured to count you out-keep it for Larry an' me. But I need help." Gorman said impatiently, "What you got. Greg, Lay it on the line."

Miller didn't give in easily. "He's got nothin' but that stinkin' star, an' I'm going to blow it right through his gut's! God, how I hate a lawman!" Just the same, at Gorman's gesture, he reluctantly put up his rifle. "Hold it, Will you? This better be good," Gorman warned Greg. Greg shook his head, "First, Larry. If you've done anything to Larry . . .!"

Gorman said petulantly, "He's all right. We left him sleeping' in camp." Greg studied him and figured he could be telling the truth. "Spit it out. Where's all the loot coming from?" Miller demanded.

"Heard about the Lazy *S* spread?" Greg asked. "No." "I was just out there looking it over." Miller spat sarcastically. "Figurin' to quit lawin' an' take up ranching'?" "Let him talk, won't you?" Gorman pleaded. "Go on, Greg." "Old man Brice . . . he's the owner . . . he's up at Abilene selling his stock. Over a thousand head. He's coming back in a few days . . . with cash." Gorman whistled softly. "Thousand head!" "And a couple of tough trail hands. That's where I need you." Gorman was jubilant. 'We'll handle them!" "How do we know you're not lying'?" Miller snapped out. Greg shrugged.

"Take a look at the Lazy *S* yourself. Nothin' but heifers and yearlings. Count 'em."

Gorman flipped a finger at Greg's badge. "But I still don't get the reason for this." Greg grinned. "You know a better way to hear what's going on around Chino Wells?"

"Like for instance just when this Aaron Brice is comin' back?" "Like that," Greg agreed.

Gorman whistled. "A thousand head!" "There's a catch to it, though." Gorman joy evaporated instantly. 'I knew it! I knew it! There always is!"

"Shut up! What's the catch?" Miller demanded of Greg. "I don't rightly know yet. Brices' wife hinted at something the old man's got up his sleeve. Couldn't very well seem to be pumping her." He touched the badge. "That's where this comes in. I got a coupla days, maybe, to nose around and find the gimmick." Gorman playfully polished the badge with his sleeve. "Say, now that's usin' the old bean!" his hand encountered something. "What's this?"

He pulled the roll of greenbacks out of Greg's vest pocket. Greg, alarmed, made a grab for the money.

"Here, give me that!" Gorman held the bills out of his reach. "We'll just keep it on account!" Greg's fist balled up, his arm raked around, and his knuckles caught Gorman on the temple. Gorman fell heavily, the bills flying out of his hand. Miller watched the quick altercation, not moving, his eyes heavily lidded, the rifle cradled in his arm. He had been appraising Greg for ten minutes now and still couldn't say he'd figured the big man out.

But when Greg bent down to pick up the money, the rifle swung to a menacing level.

"Leave it lay." Greg looked up from the ground and saw the rifle. He dropped the bills in his hand, then straightened up slowly. He spoke carefully, conscious of the finger on the rifle's trigger. "The money's not mine." Miller grunted and spat. "You never said a truer word, partner." Gorman, sprawled on the ground, watched the two. Greg, motionless for a long moment, came to life. He turned his back on Miller and headed for his horse.

Gorman scrambled to his feet. "Greg, where you goin'?" Greg prepared to mount.

"Getting' Larry and movin' out." Gorman rubbed his temple. "What's the idea?" he asked querulously. Greg said, "I don't want to be tied up to a couple of galoots with meat blocks where their heads ought to be." "Now look here . . ." Gorman began. Greg, looking down at them from the height of the big roan, took the badge off his shirt and threw it to the dirt between them. "You can take this back to Chino Wells. Or wear it yourself. I won't be needing it any more." It was Miller who put a hand on the horse's bridle and said, "Hold it, Farley." And when Greg said nothing: "What's on your mind?"

"Mrs. Brice gave me that money to pay a feed bill in town for her. If I don't pay it, I'm through in Chino Wells." Gorman and Miller looked at each other. "He's right," Gorman said. Miller hesitated. "Pick up the money, Gorman. The badge too." Greg waited impassively in the saddle until Gorman handed him the greenbacks and the badge. He took them without comment, wheeled his mount about and disappeared down the switchback.

Gorman and Miller stood looking after him until the sound of hoofbeats faded into the rustle of the thin breeze. Gorman felt he had to say something to justify himself. "It'd be stupid to pass up a big chance for a few buck's." "Maybe," Miller said slowly.

"But I can't help gaggin' at workin' with a lawman." "He ain't a lawman!" "He looks like one. The way he fought for that dinero, he even smells like one." "You don't have to worry about Farley. He'll play along." Miller turned his back and headed for his own horse. When he spoke, it was with grim meaning. "If he knows what's good for that brother of his, he will."

Steven E. Farley

Chapter 8

A Few scrawny chickens scratched a precarious living in front of the unpainted shack.

There was not another dwelling in sight; this must be Bill Moody's home. But the pinto pony tethered outside was clearly out of place there. Greg tugged the roan's bridle off the path and dismounted next to the pinto. The sound of someone chopping wood came to him, he walked around the side of the shack,

Gary was swinging an axe as big as him self, manfully but without visible effect on a tough, knotty section of cottonwood stump. A pang shot through Greg. He saw another pipe stemmed kid fighting that axe. The remembered ache went through his shoulders and arms. As the axe reached the top of its swing, he lifted it from the boy's hands. Gary whirled about. "Mr. Farley." Grinning at him, Greg swung the axe. The blade bit deep into the cottonwood, riving it neatly in two. He was setting the parts up when another voice stopped him. "Come and get it. Gary!" Jessica appeared at the door of the shack.

The sleeve protectors were gone, an' apron half covered her billowing skirt. Her face was flushed, and a wisp of raven hair had escaped its prime imprisonment. A skillet in her hand completed the transformation. She was clearly taken aback at seeing him. A quick unconscious flirt of her hand magically caught and subdued the wayward hair; another wiped away the wrinkles of her skirt. "Oh, Mr. Farley." She recovered, and smiled warmly at him. "Won't you join us? We were sitting down to dinner."

"Yeah," Gary seconded. "Miss. Jessica's a good cook, Mr. Farley. Almost as good as Pa." Jessica smiled. "And that's high praise, believe me!" Greg allowed Gary to lead him inside the shack. It was a poor place, reflecting the rough and ready care of a home without a woman. But Jessica had put a gay cloth on the table, and had brought other touches to the service. A big basket with a checkerboard towel showed where the provisions came from. Delicious, mouth-watering smells came from the stove.

"Coffee, Mr. Farley." Gary held up his cup, too. "I've got milk for you, young man."

Gary's scream was mortified. "Milk! That's for babies!" Jessica looked at Greg helplessly. "Tell him, Mr. Farley. Tell him coffee's bad for him. He won't listen to me."

"Maybe I'm not the one to talk, Greg said. "Been drinking it myself since I was two." Gary roared, and Jessica eyes flashed. "Well, *you're* a big help!" Shaking her head, she poured the black liquid into Gary's waiting mug. "That's the stuff! Good and strong." Gary smacked his lips. He spooned sugar into the cup.

"I've asked him to come and stay with us until his father . . ." Jessica hesitated. "That is, for a while." "No, sir," Gary said resolutely. "I can get along fine." "See what you can do with him, Mr. Farley. You have influence, it seems."

It was a new role for Greg. He made an awkward attempt to comply. "You ought to do what Miss Jessica says, Gary."

Gary shook his head scornfully. "Uh-uh. I run the place myself most of the time, when Pop's hittin' the bottle." "Just the same, a fellow needs somebody to take care of him."

"Who takes care of *you*?" Gary asked. "Mr. Farley means somebody in your size,"

Jessica told him sharply. "I'm practically growed! I'm twelve!" "Just the same, wish I'd had an offer like that at your age." "Did your pop hit the bottle, too?" "He died when I was a sprout." The boy showed quick concern. "Your mom?"

"The next year. So, you see, kid, I know what it means to be dragged up. And believe me, it ain't good." "Didn't you have nobody?" Gary asked sympathetically. "A kid brother. I can remember him at your age. He was just as ornery as you are. Miss Jessica givin' you a real break. Better jump at it, Gary." "Nope, Pop expects me to look after the place. He'd be disappointed if I wasn't here when he got out." Jessica threw up her hands in humorous resignation.

"Afraid I can't compete with Pop! Maybe he gives lessons in charm." After, dinner, Jessica started to clear up, but Gary sprang to his feet. "Now you don't have to wash up, Miss Jessica. I'll do that!" Jessica stood by helplessly as Gary whisked the dishes out of her hands and bustled to the sink. Greg stood up. "Thanks for the meal, Gary."

Gary turned from his industrious pumping. "Don't thank me, Mr. Farley. Miss Jessica, she brung the grub, an' cooked it too!"

"I'll be gettin' along," Greg said. "You've got to let me help, Gary," Jessica offered once more. "Not on your tintype!" "Gary! What a way to talk!" Gary laughed. "That's what Pop says. But you don't have to stick around. I can take care of everything." Jessica gave Greg a what-can-you-do-with-a-kid-like-this expression. She went up to Gary and squeezed him affectionately. "All right, Gary; I know when I've worn out my welcome.

Now you be sure and eat, understand? And if you need anything, you know where to find me." Gary ducked the caress self-consciously. 'Sure do, Miss Jessica. Thanks again!"

He grinned impishly at Greg. "So long, Mr. Farley!"

Chapter 9

They walked to their horses in silence for a moment. Then Jessica said: "Did you really?" "Really what?" 'Drink coffee when you were two?" "Afraid so. Did a lot of other things you wouldn't expect a kid to do. Does that shock you?" "I guess not. You were dragged up, you said." "Mother died year after Larry was born. I was six."

He help her mount, then mounted himself. She turned the pinto's head toward town, and Greg followed suit. "We lived with a farmer till he beat Larry. We ran away. My father was killed . . ." The next words came out without his volition. "By a sheriff's posse."

"Why do you tell me that?" she asked quietly. "I don't know. I never told anybody before." "Nobody here is going to judge you by what your father was or did." She hesitated. "Is that why you took the badge? I wondered." Greg frowned. "It's a job. I needed the money." "A lot of men in town need the money. But the job went begging. No one would take it, except the kind of man we wouldn't want." Greg squirmed inwardly under her perception that laid him bare. "You don't know anything about me. How do you know I'm the kind . . ." Jessica smiled. "Are you trying to tell me you to have a bad reason for doing a good thing?

59

There are people like that, you know." Greg kept silent. "Yesterday you were looking at Gary, talking to his father through the jail window. That was when you changed your mind and took the badge. You saw another boy there, didn't you? Not Gary; you."

Her words took his mind back to the nightmare years ago in the shack filled with the acrid sting of burnt powder and bursting with the thunder of Earl Farley's guns, louder than life in the tiny enclosure; to that other Greg, a skinny, terrified ten-year-old, huddled in a corner with his arm about his little brother Larry, trying even then to still the younger boy's quaking.

The look in Earl Farley's face came back to him, a cornered animal, breathing hate through clenched teeth as he sought to pinpoint and silence the barking guns that tore savage splinters through the puncheon planks, seeking a deadly home in his body. The shudder that shook Earl Farley's and his grunt as a slug bit into him.

To his dying day, Greg would never lose these memories. Nor the picture' of Earl Farley, turning to the two boys, blood streaming over his eye, nor the words he spat out at them. "Respectable folks! You see this, Greg? This is what respectable folks can do! I don't want you to forget it, ever! You hear me? *Don't ever forget it*!"

Then beefy men had burst into the cabin from all sides, it seemed, pumping unnecessary slugs into Earl Farley's already dead body. And the biggest of the bunch had turned, his thatched eyebrows rising. "What d'ye know! He had his kids here!"

That was the one with the badge. Larry, all of four years old, flung himself forward, beating at the man's knees. "You leave my daddy alone, you dirty *sheriff*!" Greg's breath came hard at the bitter, searing memory. He was angry with the girl for bringing it all back; he spoke more harshly than he intended. "Do you always take people apart to see what makes them tick?"

"Only when I'm interested," she said quietly. Greg stared straight ahead. The trim white gate of the Lazy *S* loomed on front of them.

"Gary wasn't the only one I was looking at then." He emphasized his meaning, running his eyes over her body. He was glad to see that she could still blush. She pulled the pinto up at the gate. "Won't you come in? I'd sure like you to meet my mother." It was Greg's turn to be flustered. "You live here?"

"Yes, of course." "You-you're a Brice? You're Aaron Brice's daughter?" "I thought you knew." "Nobody told me." He recovered. "I've met your mother." "Oh? You'll meet dad in a couple of days. You'll like Dad. And he'll be mighty glad to see you." "Me?" he said.

"He's been hollerin' for a sheriff for Chino Wells since I don't know when." "Oh," Greg said. Her whole face lighted up at the mention of her father. It was a little like the way Gary's face lighted up when he spoke of the bleary wreck of a man who had sired him; the way another boy had swelled with pride to be touched or noticed by a man who died, bleeding from half a dozen wounds, in a dark shack many years gone.

"Mother worries about him on these trips." Jessica was saying. "But not me. Dad's got a kind of system . . ." Suddenly Greg didn't want to hear any more, not from her. He cut in sharply: 'Guess I'd better be getting' back to town."

Steven E. Farley

"Sure you won't come in just for a minute?" He shook his head and touched his hat.

"Thanks, no. You'll excuse me?" She watched the roan whip about and gallop away at the touch of his knee' watched the straight back under the jacket that stretched tightly over broad shoulders.

Then he was gone, and slowly she turned the pinto's head through the white gate.

Chapter 10

The fire burned low; it was no protection against the chill wind that whistled down from the high peaks. But Larry had weighed the discomfort against the effort of gathering more wood and had made up his mind. Or rather, his mind was made up' for him by the throbbing pain in his side. He pulled the sweat- and dung-smelling horse blanket closer about the sheepskin jacket and buried his face in its musty folds.

The crackling of the brush nearby jerked him out of even this haven; he reached for the gun close to his hand, tightening his already cold-numb fingers about the chilled steel. It was Greg, he was pretty sure, but he weren't taking any chances. Greg came though the brush, a bag in his hand. Larry lowered the gun and grumbled, "Greg. Thought you'd never get here."

Greg opened the bag. "More grub for you. How you feelin', Larry?" "Some better. Not much." "That pain killer workin'?" "It's the waitin' around that hurts. But it won't be long now, will it, Greg? The boys told me . . ."

Greg stepped on his eagerness. 'I wanted to talk to you about that, kid." Larry showed quick concern.

"Something gone wrong?" "Kind of. Larry, we're pullin' out." "We are?"

Greg nodded curtly. "The job's off." "But I don't get it. The boys said . . ."

'The boys don't need to know. It's just you and me." Greg leaned forward persuasively.

"We'll make the border; you'll be safe . . . " Larry's tone went hard. "An' leave that soft touch for Gorman and Miller?" "It's not as soft as all that." "You're sure changin' your tune, Greg." Larry eyed his brother narrowly.

"And what if I am! It's you I'm thinking about, Larry." Larry said fiercely. "An' me, I'm thinkin' about that money!" "There'll be other jobs when you're better." Larry cut him short. "Pie in the sky! We're takin' this one." He broke off. "You're turnin' yellow!"

Greg didn't answer. Larry half-sat, ignoring the pain. "Was a time you wouldn't take that-even from me." "What do you want me to do-hit a sick man?" Greg's voice showed the strain he labored under.

"Maybe you ain't got the guts even for that," Larry rasped out viciously. Greg swallowed his fury, forcing himself to speak gently. "We've always leveled with each other, Larry. When I tell you this just won't work out . . . What's the matter?"

Larry had suddenly let out a gasp of pain and sank back. "Greg, help me! It hurts! It hurts like fire." He was a little boy again, clasping his hurt and calling on his big brother.

Greg bent down toward him. "Let me see. It's bleeding' again. And it looks angry. You gotta see a doctor."

"No, Greg! He'll ask questions." Greg pointed to his badge. "I'm the sheriff down there. I'll answer 'em."

He picked Larry up in his arms. Larry looked at him and managed a smile. "When I was a shaver and stubbed my toe or something, you used to carry me like this." Greg said nothing; just lifted him to the roan's back.

"I ain't worth it, Greg. Why don't you just cut loose from me? Why didn't you do it all these years?"

"Keep quiet an' save your strength." Greg had a sudden thought. He went back to the campfire and picked up the saddle blanket that Larry had been using for a comforter, then came back to the roan.

"Take off that sheepskin," he said. Larry, wrapped up in his own pain, was querulous. What for?" Greg threw it open and showed Larry the initials burned into the lining.

"They knew Fuller down in Chino. We don't want them askin' questions. Here, I'll help you." Larry shucked the jacket. Greg threw it over by the fire and tucked the saddle blanket around Larry.

The younger man shivered as they started down the slop. "You think of everything, don't you, brother?"

Greg carefully masked his expression as Dr. Brown leaned over Larry on the black leather couch and expertly removed the caked and dirty bandage from the boy's wound.

Without raising his eyes from his work, Brown asked, How'd he get this, Farley?" He couldn't have noticed Greg's infinitesimal pause. "Don't know yet. He's not in much shape to talk." "Um. No. I reckon not." Doc said in a low voice. Greg's brows moved together slightly. "Think you'll pull him around, Doc?"

"Hard to say. This slug should've been removed days ago." He reached for a probe.

"Depends how deep the poison . . . Here, hold him down, will you, Sheriff? I don't want him to jerk around." Gritting his teeth hard inside pursed, tight lips, Greg held Larry's shoulders to the couch and watched the jaws of the probe disappear into the red-black hole in Larry's flesh, then move about, reaching, searching. Doc grunted with satisfaction. "Got it." He drew out the slug and let it clatter to the floor, "Hand me that swab, will you?"

A minute later he taped the clean bandage in place. "Nothing to do now until he wakes up. That might be hours . . . or never." Again Greg held the mask of his face steady. Brown looked into the sleeping face.

"Just a kid," he mused. "But a kid with a gun can be as big as a man, can't he, Sheriff?" Greg permitted himself a grunt. "This one wasn't." Brown laved his hands in the basin.

"No, he wasn't." A commotion of angry voices outside drew both their heads around. Greg went to the window and looked out. Down in the street, a dozen men milled about in a tight knot, their unintelligible shouts lacing the air like sharp spurts of gunfire.

Doc Brown was beside him, his hands still wet and soapy. "Guess I'd better check into it, Doc." Greg said. He glanced at the still figure on the couch. "Take care of him for me."

"He won't get away." Brown assured him. "And I'll let you know when he can talk." Already at the door, Greg nodded.

The men were too excited to notice him as he pushed his way to the center of the knot. Three men were holding tightly to a fourth; a thin, scared youth who hadn't been shaving six months, by Greg's estimate. He stared, wide-eyed and slack-mouthed, from one to the other, as if he understood the excitement no more than Greg did, although he was aware he was the cause of it. There was something about the youth that was reminiscent of Larry; Greg did not immediately place what it was.

Ray Tuttle stood near the men who held the youth. He took Greg's arm.

"Sheriff! Glad you got here." "What's all this?" Greg asked. Half dozen men talked at once. Greg caught only a few words; but they were enough to jerk him to quick, ramrod alertness.

"This is Marshal . . . Fuller's . . . dirty killer." Tuttle held up his hand for silence.

"This is one of 'em, Mr. Farley; one of the men we' been watching for. Probably the one who bushwhacked Marshal Fuller himself."

"I never bushwhacked nobody!" the scared youth protested in a surprisingly high, thin voice. "I don't know what all this is about, I swear it!"

"Shut up!" growled the man who held his left arm; while on the other side his captor contented himself with a backhand slap across the young man's mouth. Greg stepped forward quickly. "None of that." he commanded "I'll take charge. Let him go."

The two captors reluctantly dropped their hold; the youth shook arms half-numbed from their iron grip. Greg turned to Tuttle "Now what makes you think this man had anything to, to do with it?"

"Look at that jacket!" Tuttle pointed. "He's wearing Marshal Fuller's windbreaker!"

"That's a lie!" the youth screamed. "I don't know, no marshal. This here's my jacket-always has been!" Greg's brows narrowed. "Common enough coat," he said, puzzled.

"There's dozen like it right here in town." "Not like this one! Take a look, Sheriff!" The nearest man whirled the youth about roughly, poking a finger through a small round hole in the back between the shoulder blades. "That's where Glenn Fuller got it-right in the back!"

"Your crazy!" the victim cried out. "I tole you a dozen times how come that bullet hole got there!" "Tell me," said Greg quietly. "It was Archie-Archie Winston. He done it-just kind of skylarkin', he was. He didn't mean no harm. It was a-hangin' on a tree limb at the time," he added almost unnecessarily. "Who's Archie Winston?"

"Feller I met up with. Kind of crazy, he was. Nobody but a crazy man would do a stunt like that-shoot a hole through a man's good fleece coat."

"Where is he now?" Greg asked. "How should I know? I'm well shet of him-crazy coot like that. I was glad to see the last of him."

"Haw!" Somebody said. "Likely story." "I don't know." Greg said, keeping his voice low and mild. "It's just loco enough to be the truth." He turned to the boy. "Which way'd this Winston go?" The youth waved a vague hand. "I dunno. Up north some'res." He shrugged his shoulders. "Jest met up with him, like I told you, an' I sure don't expect never to see him no more."

"Well, you better pull him out of your hat." Came a familiar voice from the sidelines,

"Or you won't be needin a hat no more-or a windbreaker, neither." "Not where you're going'!" another voice added. Greg glanced that way. It was Morgan, all right. Greg hushed the guffaws this inspired. "That's something for a judge to decide," he said sternly. He thought of something that hadn't seemed important up to now. "What's your name, son?"

"Pullman, Red Pullman." Greg glanced automatically at his hair. There wasn't much red in it; just enough of a glint remaining to justify a kid nickname that hung on regardless. He took the boy's arm. "Come along, Pullman. "We'll get you away from all this, anyway."

"Why put it off?" Morgan called out. "We can get it over here and now!" Greg wheeled on him and fixed him with his eyes. "None of that, Morgan," he said quietly. "I don't want to hear that kind of talk, now or ever." Just the same, he was well aware of other assenting murmurs from men following Morgan's lead.

Several of the men started to follow Greg and Pullman. He ignored them, but the boy turned about fearfully. "Eyes front." Greg commanded him. "Pay no attention to them."

Pullman obeyed. Greg could feel the thin arm tremble in his grip. As they neared the office, Pullman held back. "You puttin' me in *jail*?" "That's right, Pullman." The youth stared, unbelieving, at the forbidding iron bars as they went through the door.

"I ain't never been in no jail before," he said wonderingly. "It's not so bad," Greg said. He got the key ring from the desk drawer, opened the cell door and stared down at Bill Moody, snoring on the only pad. He frowned. "Wait a minute," he told Pullman. The water bucket hung near at hand. Greg removed the dipper and splashed the contents of the bucket into Moody's face. Moody spluttered his way to wakefulness "What th' devil!" His eyes opened, and he saw Greg standing over him.

"Think you're sobered up enough to go home, Moody?" Moody looked at the open door, at the boy standing outside it. "You're turning me loose?" "I'm releasing you on your own recognizance. When the circuit judge gets here, you come back and stand trial."

Moody shaking his dripping head; stunned. "Golly Mr. Farley, I don't know what to say!" "Nothing to say. Get on home." Moody looked at Pullman. "Oh. What you done, kid?" "I never done nothin'," Pullman said. "All right," Greg interrupted. "Save it, Bill."

He waved Pullman inside the door and locked it. Bill Moody, still unable to believe his good fortune, stood halfway to the door, hat in hand. "Gosh, Mr. Farley," he said again and again. Greg cut in on him. "You take good care of that boy-understand?"

"Oh, I will, I will!" "And, Bill . . . " "Yes, Mr. Farley?" "If I hear of you touching a bottle, I'm going to come out and finish the job I started on you. That's a promise."

Moody gave him a twisted grin, wiping the drops of water from his hair before putting on the hat. "You can count on me, Sheriff! I won't let you down!" I won't let you down!"

He touched his hat brim in awkward gratitude and sidled out of the door. Greg looked at the keys that jingled in his hand for a moment, replaced them in the desk drawer and sat down heavily. He was conscious of the burning eyes following his every move from behind the bars. The boy spoke finally, hesitantly. "Sheriff." "Yes?" "What's gonna happen to me?" "You heard me tell Bill Moody. Judge'll be ridin' in three-four days from now. You'll have your hearing." "What if the judge don't believe me?" "Somebody from Sedona will be up to identify you at the trial. You got nothing to worry about." The boy seized on a thin strand of hope. "You don't believe I done it, do you, Sheriff?'

Greg caught himself. "I got no way of knowin'," he said. Pullman's disappointment was as quick as his hope had been. "You *sounded* like you didn't believe it." Greg frowned.

"Ain't up to me." He stood up. "Better pass me that jacket, son." "What for?"

"Evidence." Reluctantly, Pullman passed it to him through the bars. Greg examined the bullet hole. What a crazy fluke! On a sudden thought, Greg turned to the front of the thick jacket. There were no burned initials there, of course.

Somebody who knew Marshall Fuller would remember those initials. He felt better. not a lot better, but some.

Steven E. Farley

Chapter 11

Greg had his midday meal at the Bailey house. It was more expensive than the widow Emanuel's chili parlor across the street; but here he had credit against his first pay-day.

From the window of the dining room, Greg could see Dr. Brown's office across the street. Behind that quiet window lay Larry. Greg had to keep himself under restraint not to go up to see Larry, to find out how he was doing. But he couldn't afford talk-particularly from Brown, who already looked askance at Greg and everything he stood for.

He remembered the face but not the name of the man who threaded his way between the tables. "Sheriff." Greg looked up. "You better come right away, Sheriff. Morgan talkin' lynch over at the Satin Slipper." Greg chewed and swallowed a mouthful of tough beefsteak before he answered. "Be over soon's I finish my dinner."

"Sure, sure." His informant said. He was properly impressed, Greg could see. The word would get around fast that the sheriff didn't put too urgent a price tag on Morgan or anything he said.

Several other diners had heard the conversation. For their benefit, Greg slowed down his eating even more. When he had mopped the last drop of white gravy from his plate, he signed the check and reached for his hat. Every eye in the place followed him out.

Morgan, with his side-kick Hobbs, was holding forth in the saloon. He had an audience of maybe a dozen, the scum of the town, Greg realized with a single sweeping glance; but even this early in the day they were liquored up enough to cause trouble.

"I remember old Judge Jenkins." Morgan's voice boomed out above the knot of men at the bar. "Soft. You know that." There was a murmur of assent from the group. Morgan, like any demagogue, made no effort to prove his assertion. "Get a man dead to rights, an' what happens? Goes scot-free."

"That's right, Morgan!" It was Hobbs, going a Johnny-on the-spot obbligato to the bigger man's refrain. "That's right. You're shore right," the chorus came in on schedule.

The bartender had a worried face that lit up with relief when he spotted Greg. "Mister Sheriff!" he called out loud enough for all to hear. A dozen faces whipped around; a way opened up magically between Greg and Morgan. Greg looked over the group, a slow, appraising look that gave each man the uneasy impression that his face was stamped indelibly on the brain behind those steady gray eyes.

Morgan's twisted smile was far from uneasy. Greg knew the hardcase looked forward to this encounter, enjoyed it. He was the kind of man Greg had come across often; but he'd never grown to relish the experience. There was the time, years ago, when he'd saved Larry from a Rattle-snake on the Escalante desert. A quick well-placed slug had halted

74

the repulsive-looking beast, turned it into a squirming, nauseating mess of blood, scales and torn tissue. The picture came before Greg's eyes now, and his gut retched with the same old disgust.

"It's the sheriff!" Morgan sneered. "Glad to see you, Sheriff. You drinking?" He turned to the bartender. "Set the sheriff up, Ollie. He can't turn us down this time. He ain't got a drink in the other hand now."

"I'm on duty." Greg reminded him. "Don't you forget it." Morgan spread out innocent hands. "Just talkin', Sheriff. No law against a man talking' with his friends, is there now?"

"Depends on the talk." Greg said. He turned on his heel and walked out. He could feel rather than hear Morgan's laugh boring into his back.

He walked back across the street to the Bailey house, went upstairs and knocked on Colonel Bailey's door. The mayor admitted him, stripped to long-sleeved gray undershirt and sock feet. "Sorry to interrupt your nap, Colonel," Greg said. "Not at all, Mr. Farley; glad to see you any time." Bailey boomed out heartily. "No trouble, I hope?" "Not yet,"

Greg said. "But that man Morgan blowin' up a storm over at the saloon. Thought you ought to know about it." "Morgan?" Bailey made a visible effort to place the name and finally succeeded. "Oh, yes. One of Brice's, men. I know him. Bad actor; what's he up to?" "Like I said, nothing yet. Nothing I can put a stop to, because so far it's just talk. What I want to know is, have you ever had a lynching in this town?"

"Lynching? Good God, no!" The mayor was really startled now. "What on earth you reaching for, anyway, son?" Greg asked another question instead of answering the one put to him. "You figure the town could get het up enough to pull something like that?"

"They'd have to have pretty strong provocation, stronger'n I can figure . . ." "They think we've got Marshal Fuller's killer." Greg told him. "Marshal-!" The mayor's face went blank. "You got the dirty rat who-?" "Now hold on, Colonel." Greg cut in. "I said they *think* he's the man. I've got him in jail." Bailey got hold of himself with an effort. 'You had me jumpin' there for a minute, boy." He wiped his sweating face. "You know we thought a heap of Marshal Fuller in this town." "So I gather." Greg said dryly. "That's what worried me." "How d'ye mean? It's only the riffraff talkin' biggety. You can handle them, can't you, Farley?" "Ray Tuttle was right up there. Also several other men who'd fight if you called 'em riffraff." Bailey took a step closer and peered into his eyes.

"What you trying to tell me? That respectable people'd back such a play?" "Respectable is just a word," said Greg. "I don't put too much stock in it." "It's just talk." Bailey said.

"It'll simmer down." "I hope so. If it don't, I'm goin to need backing." "You'll get it," said Bailey confidently. "You just got through telling me Marshal Fuller was well liked around here." "What's that got to do with it?" Greg studied the older man before he said. "Will you answer a question for me?" "Sure Farley." "If you were pretty well convinced this man was Marshal Fuller's killer, would you take up a rifle to stop a lynching?" "I'm mayor here. I'm bound to uphold the law." But Bailey's split-second hesitation was answer enough, and they both knew it. Bailey broke the silence that followed. "You sure this man is innocent?" it was Greg's turn to hesitate. "He tells a story that's going to be hard to prove. Sounds windy, to listen to it. But it could be true." He told Bailey about the jacket with the bullet hole in it.

Bailey's relief was evident. 'A downright lie if I ever heard one! Shootin' holes in a jacket for the fun of it!" "That's for a jury to decide, Colonel." Greg reminded him. "Oh. Naturally, naturally, Farley. You can count on me. You can count on all the good people in this town." His voice had a hollow ring. Greg nodded and said. "Fine. Let's round 'em up."

Bailey looked blank. "Round 'em-?" Greg nodded curtly. "I'll wait for you." Wondering, the Colonel reached for his boots.

As they came out of the Bailey house, the Colonel glanced toward the Satin Slipper, baking in the desert noon.

"Looking mighty quiet." he commented. "Want to go and listen?" Greg asked him. Bailey hesitated. "No, I guess not. Let's get over to the bank."

Greg jerked a thumb, and Bailey's eyes followed it. From north and south men were drifting toward the saloon as to a magnet. Not many men, Here and there a loafer ceased his whittling and detached himself from a store-front chair; a waddy carelessly threw rein over the hitching post and clattered his high heels up the two steps to the boardwalk. Two men put heads together at a corner and started across the hot street in the sun.

"Riffraff." Bailey said. "A gun don't care who pulls its trigger." Greg answered laconically.

"An' a rope don't ask for a social reference." Bailey pursed his lips.

Chapter 12

The riffraff started it, Greg thought to himself. They could be handled even with a man like Morgan at their head. But when the responsible element of the town wasn't firmly planted in their path, ready to risk danger and even death to uphold the law, a sheriff was helpless. Greg had seen it happen before.

His thoughts went to the scared boy behind bars. The crazy kid! To come into that town, on that day, with that unbelievable story about a loco trail mate shooting holes in a windbreaker! Greg didn't blame Bailey. In the mayor's boots, maybe he couldn't have believed the kid's story, either.

But he had to find help enough to stand up to Morgan, stop him in his tracks, discourage the half-convinced mob that would follow him, or there would be tragedy. One man couldn't handle it. Sure, Greg had heard all the stories about a single man with determination turning back a lynch-bent mob, but he knew them for the legends they were. It didn't work that way; and the few brave souls who'd tried it just got trampled down for their foolhardiness. Three good men with shotguns, yes. Even two might have an outside chance, but not one.

Greg's first thought was for Jessica as they entered the bank. He threw a quick glance around. She wasn't there. Relieved, he followed Bailey to Barker's desk.

They didn't have to tell Barker the story. He'd seen the whole thing through the bank window. He'd seen the fleece-lined jacket and the bullet hole, too; and he was sold on Pullman's guilt. But he didn't want there to be a lynching on the town's conscience.

"Good," Greg said. "Send out a couple of your people and round up some men to help."

"How many?" "The more the better. The mayor here can deputize them." Barker hesitated. "Deputize" had the metallic, official sound of harsh reality. "You think this thing is honestly that? I mean, you think Morgan will really start some thing?"

"Time to stop it is before it gets started. That way nobody gets hurt. Those whiskey tramps see a dozen men with rifles on the street, and they'll get religion fast."

"Hmmm," said Barker. "Guess you're right, Where you want to meet-at your office?"

Greg thought it over. No use scaring Pullman half to death. "Will here be all right with you?" "Sure thing!" Barker stood up. "How soon do you want them?"

Greg looked out of the window. Across the street, two more men were pushing into the batwings at the Satin Slipper. "Morgan surely won't do anything until he gets more men around him," Bailey said.

"Let's not count on it," Greg replied. Barker called over two of his clerks and gave them brief instructions. "Keep separated," Greg added, "and keep casual. Won't do for that gang to get wind of what you're doing." One man went out the back way, mounted and rode to the far end of town, while the other moved casually, as if on bank business, and disappeared into one of the side streets to alert the merchants.

"Greg stood up. "Where you going?" Bailey asked. "My prisoner has to eat," Greg said.

"I'll be back." He went out into the parched street, crossing again to the Bailey House. He kept his head averted from the saloon, yet was perfectly conscious of the eyes that followed his progress through the windows from the darkened interior.

Emerging from the Bailey House restaurant with a covered tray, he had to pass in front of the saloon once more. The swinging doors moved slightly, and a gun barked fire from inside. The tin tray clanged like a penny arcade target as the slug took it out of Greg's hands and scattered bread, meat, and coffee in the street.

Raucous laughter came from the saloon, but no faces showed. Greg stood still for a long second, the tingling shock still traveling up his arm. Then he turned and headed straight into the Satin Slipper.

Morgan and Hobbs were at the rear, leaning against the bar as if planted there from the year one. The half-dozen other men lolled in similarly self-conscious attitudes, elaborately paying no attention to the entering sheriff. Greg looked over the situation. He went to the bartender, elaborately polishing a clean glass behind the mahogany.

"Who did it?" Greg demanded. The bartender raised his eyebrows. "Did what, Sheriff?"

He wasn't in on the rawhide; Greg could tell that from the fear that trembled behind his eyes. He was taking the safe way out; he'd made up his mind; who could hurt him the most and the fastest. There was no use counting on him, Greg knew.

"Checking your shotgun," he barked. Slowly the bartender brought the weapon up from below the counter and offered it to Greg. Greg broke the breech, then looked sharply at the man. "It's empty." The bartender made a bad job of pretending surprise. "Well, what d'ye know!" "Better load it up," Greg advised. The bartender looked beneath the counter again and came up empty-handed.

"Seems I misplaced the shell," he said unconvincingly. Greg was conscious of the grins boring into his back. The longer he stayed there, the more face he lost. "Well, get some," he ordered. "Yes, *sir!*" "Yes, *sir*, Sheriff!" It was Morgan's voice. Greg walked up to him.

Morgan had a lariat and was fashioning the end of it into a hanging knot. He held it out as Greg approached. "Pretty knot, eh, Sheriff?" Greg would have bet a horse and saddle that he'd find the bartender's shotgun shells in Morgan's pocket, if he searched. But what was the use?

Morgan turned his back on Greg deliberately. "Say, Hobbs, remember Red Fletcher an' Lem Lashley? Saw 'em in town this mornin'. Whyn't you mosey out an' find 'em?" He turned his back to Greg to make sure the explanation got across. 'Like to stand 'em to a drink."

"Sure, Morgan!" The grinning, buck-toothed Hobbs brushed by Greg. "'Scuse me, Sheriff!" He banged his way to the swinging doors, stopped and grinned foolishly at Greg.

"Who knows? Might be some fun in town tonight. Eh, Sheriff?" Greg handed the shotgun back to the bartender. "See that it's in shape next time I check." "Yes, *sir!*" said the bartender, stowing the weapon beneath the mahogany bar.

"Yes, *sir*, Sheriff!" Morgan's mocking voice followed Greg out the doors.

Bailey and Barker were in the bank when Greg reentered, but there were no other men beside the two tellers. "What's the matter?" Greg asked, going up to the banker and the mayer. "I don't know," Barker said in a worried tone. "I sure don't know, Farley."

"Well, I do," Bailey boomed out, More loudly than necessary. "They didn't show because they ain't got no heart for this business."

Greg looked at him, surprised. "No heart to head off a lynching?" Bailey avoided his gaze. Marshal Fuller was a powerful popular man around Chino Wells."

"I'm getting a little tired of that line." Greg said dryly.

"What you're saying is, a lot of the men you'd count on as deputies'd rather be on the other side, if it came to a showdown." Barker said belligerently. "Lot of folks ain't partial to helpin' the skunk that shot him in the back."

"They already decided he's the one that did it." Greg pronounced flatly. "Is that what you're sayin'?"

"There's that sheepskin." Barker said. "An' the bullet hole in the back. Saw that with my own eyes."

"You *want* a lynching in this town?" They averted their eyes. "No." Bailey said finally.

"No, of course not." "You're against lynching, but not too much against it." Greg said.

"Is that it?" Greg went up to the tellers who had tried to round up deputies. "Who' all'd you talk to?" he asked.

The men glanced at their employer before answering. Barker nodded. "You can tell him. No secret."

The men named a dozen names that meant nothing to Greg. "What about Doc Brown?" he asked. "You invite him?" The two tellers looked at each other. "Never thought of him, somehow," one of them said.

"Doc's queasy about violence, anyway." Barker told Greg. "Easy to understand why he'd slip a man's mind." "Just asking." Greg said. "I wondered."

"He'd have come for this!" It was Jessica, who had somehow come in without their noticing her. Her eyes flashed. "He'd have come a lot sooner than some of the biggety talkers around this town, to judge from results."

"Now, Miss Jessica." Barker placated. "Nobody's tryin' to say . . ." Jessica paid no attention to him. Her eyes were all for Greg. "What about it, Mr. Farley? You really expect trouble?" Greg hesitated. "Morgan's sure spoilin' over there."

"Then why didn't you do something? Arrest him?" "You can't pull a man in for talkin'. I have to wait till he makes his play." "And that will be too late!" Greg was silent for a moment. He turned to Bailey. "Colonel, how'd you get your rank? Union army?"

Bailey drew himself up and attempted the impossible feat of pulling in his stomach.

"Proud of it, proud of it!" he exclaimed. "All right. You're mayor here. You got a job to do, same as me, whether you like it or not."

"Now see here-!" spluttered Bailey. Greg ignored the outburst.

"I'm getting' out of town . . ." "What!" shouted Barker. "I'll be back in an hour. Somebody's got to see that

Morgan don't start anything for that hour." He fixed his glance on them with thinly veiled contempt. "Think you can do it?"

"Where are you going?" "Never mind. I got an idea. Rather not talk about it. I'm leavin' you with one thought. If you let Morgan grab that kid, you're lettin' an innocent man get lynched." He put on his hat and started for the door. He found his way blocked by a determined, furious, Jessica.

"You're running out!" Greg liked the fire he saw in her eyes. "Would you blame me, Miss Jessica?" She attempted to answer, but found no words. Suddenly she flushed to the lace-bordered dimity that cut off the first swelling hint of bosom beneath; she fell aside and let him go past her out the door.

Gary scattered grain from a tin pan in a wide swath about him. "Here, chickie, chickie, chickie!" He could have saved his breath. The chickens scratched and clucked, climbing over each other to get at the feed.

But suddenly there was a greater flurry than usual. Gary looked around. "Pop!" He dropped the pan and rushed unashamedly into Bill Moody's arms.

The big man patted his head awkwardly, swallowing a lump in his throat.

"Pop! You got out! What happened?" The boy had a sudden thought. "You break jail?"

Moody laughed. " 'Course not. Sheriff let me go. I gotta go back for trial. He's a good man, the sheriff is. Understands a fellow."

"He sure is! He was out here yesterday! So was Miss Jessica. I been takin' care of the place good, Pop. Come on inside; I'll show you . . ."

He dragged Moody into the cabin. "See, Pop, I even swept the floor." Moody chuckled. "First time in a coon's age that's happened!"

"Sit down, Pop. I'll get you some vittles. Miss Jessica brought 'em." Moody sat.

"Good people. Mighty good people," he murmured, the moisture dimming his sight.

Gary set a plate before him.

Chapter 13

The feel of the rough chaparral trail up the mountainside was already familiar to the roan. The big-muscled flanks between his thighs made the move to the right or left before Greg got around to pressuring them.

Frank Gorman put up his gun as he recognized Greg. "What you doin' here in broad daylight, Sheriff?" Greg threw a glance over the mess of gear and duffel that marked their untidy housekeeping. "Where's that sheepskin?" he asked. "Sheepskin?" "You know the one I mean. I made Larry leave it here when I took him down to Chino."

Gorman brows narrowed. "What you want it for?" Greg dismounted, and began turning over blankets searching for the jacket. He found it and straightened up.

"Somebody pulled in a kid for killing the marshal." Miller said. Greg whirled around.

"How'd you know that?" Miller grinned evilly. Gorman blurted out; "You double-crossing liar! You tole me you was ridin' to the top of the rise! You went to town!"

Greg reached for Miller. "I thought you'd have better sense . . ."

"Hold it, Sheriff." Miller spat out the words as a snake' spits venom. "Somebody's gotta ride herd on you. I just elected myself to the job."

Greg dropped back a step; he held his hands carefully away from his sides. "I ain't looking for trouble, Miller. I need this jacket."

"What's all this about, anyway?" Gorman whined. "Ain't you gonna let a fellow know?"

"It's just like the sheriff says." Miller filled him in. "They nabbed this kid for the marshal's job. Talkin' lynch, they are." "You don't say!" Gorman's interest was purely academic. "Like to see that; I sure would!"

"You know the kid's innocent." Greg said evenly. "I wouldn't worry if he got to a judge, but lynching-" "Best darn thing could happen!" Miller said. "You know that, Farley. Take the heat off your kid brother. Take it off for good." "Say, that's right!" Gorman concurred. "Make it easier on all of us."

"Sure." Miller said, putting up his gun. "Even the sheriff sees that, don't you, sheriff?"

"I'm taking that jacket back." Greg said. "The kid's innocent. I ain't gonna see a man lynched." "Maybe you'd rather see the guilty man lynched." Miller said. "Like to see your brother at the end of rope?" He turned to Gorman. "They'll do it, too. They liked that marshal a lot down Chino Wells way."

Greg held in his anger. "You learned a lot in a short time, didn't you?" "I got ears." His hand was moving imperceptibly toward his gun. Greg caught the motion and tensed himself, ready. "I told you I don't want trouble, Miller." He said slowly. "But if you want to make your move, make it now. I'm takin' this jacket back to Chino."

The two stood motionless, facing each other, bombs on sputtering short fuses; Gorman hung comically off-balance as he waited for the explosion, forgetting to breathe, a thread of saliva dribbling unnoticed on the corner of his mouth. And then, as suddenly as it had begun, it was over. Ben Miller sucked in his breath and relaxed his taut frame. He laughed shortly, turned his back, and kicked a branch into the fire.

Greg turned without a word, mounted, and rode off with the windbreaker on the saddle before him.

Even before he reached the outskirts of the town he could sense its changed character. There was an electric charge in the air that penetrated the very dust rising from the milling of many boots and hooves, punctuated by an occasional shout and the sting of a gunshot. Greg touched heels to the roan's flanks and leaned forward in the saddle, gripping the sheepskin in white-knuckled fingers.

Rounding the corner into the main street, he stared with surprise. He couldn't remember when he'd ever seen so many people in one place at one time. They swarmed over the boardwalks, peered out of the windows, and there must have been fifty in the knot in front of the jail itself.

Greg thundered down the hard-packed mud to the sheriff's office: but long before he reached it, cries went up.

"Sheriff!" "Mr. Farley!" "Stop them! They'll kill him!" a woman shouted out. From the corner of his eye Greg saw Bailey, Barker, with half a dozen of the towns leading people, helping the mayor hold off the mob.

Greg saw the rope, thrown over a beam in front of the Satin Slipper, ready for its victim. The door of the sheriff's office was filled by a solid pack of humanity. Greg made out the burly figure of Ray Tuttle. He was fighting; but even his bulk and great strength were out-matched by sheer numbers. He saw Greg and managed a shout before he went down.

Greg could not make out the sense of his words. There were fast hoof beats behind Greg now. He turned, went for his gun, but never made it. The horse's body crashed against the roan's, causing a stabbing pain to run up Greg's leg in the collision, and a sweaty sleeve snaked over his mouth, jerking him backward and off the saddle.

As he thudded against the ground, Greg clutched for the sheepskin jacket. It was gone, and he realized with a hollow feeling that it must be fifty feet back of him by now, ground into the dirt by a hundred unheeding boots. But even as he fell, he caught a glimpse of a figure running out of a remembered door toward the street. Arms and hands grabbed at Greg from all directions and jerked him to his feet.

"Doc!" Greg yelled. "Doc Brown!" The running figure turned, saw and heard him. Greg twisted his head as, trussed with humanity more tightly than chains, he was literally lifted off his feet and transported toward the Satin Slipper. "The jacket!" Greg tore the scream out of his rasping throat as he was carried away. "Get the jacket, Doc!"

He was turned again, and had no way of knowing whether or not his words had carried across the yells of his captors, and whether or not, if the doctor had heard, or if he understood.

Nor did he know if, understanding, he would do anything about it. Before him the noose dangled, swinging, beckoning. For a fleeting instant, the thought crossed Greg's pain-jarred mind that they were going to hang him instead of the boy. This startling impression, was quickly erased, however, by the sight of the trembling Red Pullman, also held by a dozen willing, eager hands, as if he could move, much less escape, what with the cords that bound him hand and foot.

Everybody wanted to get into the act. Later they'd brag about touching the kid before he swung; proudly display a treasured inch of the rope that had snuffed out a human life.

Pullman called out to Greg. "Sheriff, you ain't gonna let 'em! I never done it, Sheriff, I swear to God I never!"

Somebody told him roughly to shut up; somebody else made the point clearer with a backhand swipe across his mouth. And from somewhere Morgan appeared, grabbed the noose, slung it over the boy's neck and drew it tight. Greg winced with him, feeling the cruel pressure at his own throat.

Morgan swaggered up to the sheriff. "Glad you decided to come back, Sheriff. We thought we was goin' to have to run the celebration without you."

"You better call this off, Morgan." Greg warned him. "You got the wrong man." Morgan laughed loud and long. "You know, sheriff, you look mighty funny there, given' orders."

His greasy, toothy sidekick, Hobbs, led chorus of hoots that picked up the jibe. Greg watched Pullman licking the blood that trickled from the corner of his mouth and twisted his head trying to look over the mob. "I can prove it . . ."

"That's enough jawin'" growled Morgan. "Let's get on with it." But Greg scarcely heard him. Through the crowd and the dust, he saw something that lifted his heart.

Jim Brown, the sheepskin jacket in his hand, was fighting his way through. The commotion on the edge of the mob turned Morgan's head as he gripped the long end of the rope with the others, ready to pull.

"Stop." There was authority in the doctor's voice, an authority that even Greg had not been able to put into his own. Even the dregs of the town that comprised the kill-crazed mob found themselves halting to heed it. Ignoring the drawn guns that brushed his face, Brown shouldered and elbowed his way to the center, and held out the jacket.

"Look at this!" he demanded in a voice that would not be denied. "Before stringing up an innocent man, look at this!" He opened the jacket to the burned initials, literally shoving them into Moran's face.

Eyes went from the sheepskin in Brown's hands to the other jacket, still on the trussed and petrified boy. Hands turned it around, fingered the bullet hole in the center, of the back-the bullet hole with its accusing aureole of dried blood. Rude words spilled from stunned lips. "Well, I'll be blamed!" "That's the marshal's coat, all right!" "Who'd a believed it?" Only Morgan was unregenerate. "It's a trick!" he bawled out.

"You ain't lettin' 'em fool you with-" But even his voice trailed off as, one by one, the men around him melted away. Fingers clutching Greg lost their pressure and were withdrawn. Somehow, magically, the bonds disappeared from the limbs of the bound boy. "You gonna let them bamboozle you?" Morgan tried again, but with the foreknowledge of defeat in his tone.

"You gonna let the hombre who killed the marshal get away with it?" Greg, his hands freed now, caught Morgan's neckerchief and yanked his face close. "You got a whale lot of a nerve talkin' about justice, Morgan. Now you get out. Get out of this town for good.

You understand me?" Morgan knocked his hand away defiantly. "You gonna make me?" "No." said Greg. "I'm advising you. That mob you riled up might just get a notion you played 'em dirty. They might get to thinkin' how close you brought 'em to doin' something they'd regret, an' they might just get mad enough to do something about it."

He paused. "An' this time I might not be able to hold 'em back." Morgan turned and looked at the gently swaying noose.

He spat on the ground at Greg's feet and turned on his heel. "Come on, Hobbs." Shoulder to shoulder with Brown, Greg watched the two mount leather and tear out of town.

"I wanta thank you, Sheriff." It was Red Pullman, still unable to believe in his narrow escape. He turned to Brown. "You, too, mister. That took guts, what you did there."

"You all right, son?" The doctor in Brown came out. "Yeah. I'm all right, I guess. But I sure aim to make tracks out of this here town." Greg jerked his thumb toward the jail. "Your horse is right there." Pullman stood awkwardly for a moment, trying to frame words. "Well, thanks. Thanks a lot." He turned and shambled toward the hitching rail outside the sheriff's office. Greg reached up and jerked down the swinging noose.

The movement caused a shaft of pain to shoot up his side. Brown did not miss his grimace.

"You come over to the office, Sheriff. That was quite a fall you took." Greg hesitated, then nodded. The street had once more changed character, suddenly, magically. Gone

93

were the riffraff, the scum who had dominated the area a moment before. The clothes were cleaner, the hair more neatly trimmed. The men who didn't condone lynching-except something-came forward, shamefaced, and did not seem insulted when Greg and the doctor brushed by them without replying to their mumbled apologies.

"Wonder where they were a minute back." Brown remarked. Greg grunted, but said nothing. It was a new and not altogether comfortable feeling, this new kinship he felt for the morose dark young man who had so strongly opposed him' from the moment he had walked the streets of Chino.

Colonel Bailey was planted in their path; they had to stop. "Sheriff." He boomed out loudly, "In the name of the town of Chino Wells, I want to thank you publicly. Your courageous action amply justifies the faith we had in you . . ."

"This man is hurt." Brown cut through. "Can you save the campaign talk for another time, Colonel, please?"

He pushed past the mayor's ample paunch, oddly deflated now, and led Greg toward his office door.

Chapter 14

Mrs. Brice stood outside the porch door, arms folded, looking at the two men on the stoop. Morgan demanded roughly. "All I want to know is; who's been talkin' to you?"

Mrs. Brice looked at the two. "You got your pay; now get off the ranch, both of you."

"It was the skunkin' sheriff, wasn't it?" Morgan insisted. "Never you mind; you just get."

Hobbs plucked Morgan's arm. "Come on, Morgan; we ain't doin' no good here." Morgan shook him off. "Get your hands offin' me!" He took a step toward the door. "Look here, old lady; you better tell me . . ." He stopped short. Behind the stocky woman the door had opened, and Wong stood in the entrance, grinning as always-with a business like grip on the double-barreled shotgun in his hands.

Mrs. Brice said, "I'm giving you just one minute to get off my property. Now get!" The two men headed sullenly for their horses. Wong held the shotgun on them till they mounted and galloped off. Mrs. Brice turned and saw the Chinese for the first time. "Thank you, Wong." She said. "matter-of-factly. But that wasn't necessary. I can handle the likes of them. Now you put that thing up before it goes off and destroys us all." Wong bobbed his head gleefully. "Yessee! Yessee!"

Greg watched the sober, young-old face of the doctor who bent over him, touching, probing, poking. "Painful?" Brown asked. "Some. Not much." Brown straightened up.

"No bones broken. I'll give you some liniment for that hip, where you landed. Keep it from stiffening up on you." Greg nodded absently. His eyes were on the still shape lying on the black couch in the corner. Brown noticed him. "I gave him some morphine. He'll sleep awhile." Turning to his dispensary closet, he asked casually. "You said you don't know him?" "No." Greg snapped the word perhaps a little too quickly. "Why should I?"

"No reason." Brown said, offering him the bottle. "Rub this on tonight." Greg nodded his thanks and headed for the door, trying hard not to glance again at Larry. "Mr. Farley." Greg turned "Everybody was pretty excited out there."

"Reckon so." Greg's guard went up. "Nobody thought to bring up a certain question."

"What's that?" Greg asked. How you happened to put your hand on Marshal Fuller's jacket so fast."

"Are you asking?" Greg wanted to know. "No." Said Brown steadily. "But that's no guarantee somebody won't, soon as they settle down and start thinking it over."

"It's good question." Greg admitted. "Maybe you better have an answer when they get around to it."

Greg looked into the steady eyes that met his own without friendship and without fear.

"Good idea." He said in the end. "If I'm around when they think of it." He held up the bottle. "Thanks for the liniment, Doc."

Steven E. Farley

Chapter 15

Bill Moody had finished drying the dishes as Gary washed them; he looked about for something else to do that would satisfy his need to prove his rehabilitation.

Gary watched him standing in the middle of the room, aimlessly moving the salt and peppershakers from one unimportant spot on the table to another.

"Sit down, Pa. Take it easy. You had a hard time." Moody made a vague gesture.

"It ain't that, son . . ." "Sure, Pop. I Know. Here. A slug of this'll settle your nerves some." Moody turned to the proffered bottle. Slowly, compulsively, he took it from a boy, feeling grateful anticipation as he touched the coolness of the smooth glass.

For a long moment Bill Moody stood looking at the bottle, motionless. Gary pushed a cup toward him. "Go on Pop. You need it."

Suddenly Moody"s giant frame came to explosive life. He flung the bottle from him; it went through the glass window, and they heard it crash on the ground outside. Then streaks of whiskey curved across the floor and wall, marking the bottle's flight.

"I don't never want to see that stuff again!" Moody screamed. He sank into a chair. Gary sank beside him. "Gee, Pop!"

Bill gulped. "I been a mighty poor father to you, boy. . ."

"Aw, don't talk like that, Pop. You're swell!"

"You're just a kid. When you grow up and look back-" He banged the table with a heavy fist. "Things is goin' to be different, Gary, from now on. Maybe the judge'll lock me up for a couple of months, but after that . . . you'll see . . ."

They were both startled at the violent roar of a shot, very close; from the sound of it, just outside the door. They looked at each other, and with one accord hurried to the yard.

Morgan was holstering his smoking six-gun, while Hobbs held the carcass of a freshly killed chicken by the neck.

"Good shot, Morgan!" Hobbs called out. Moody blustered forward. "Blast it, what's the idea!" The knife scar on Morgan's jaw glowed bright as he recognized Moody.

"Well, if it ain't the jailbird!" Moody grabbed for the chicken, and Hobbs jerked it out of his reach, grinning. "You ain't gonna begrudge a couple of hungry men a measly little chicken, are you now, Moody?"

Morgan said, "Oh, Bill Moody is tough. I remember he was gonna wipe up the ground with the two of us, if the sheriff only let him out of jail."

"Yeah!" Hobbs grinned wider. "And what d'ya think! He's out. Maybe we better make a run for it, Morgan, before he murders us!" Red fury filmed Bill Moody's vision. His giant fist balled up and caught the unwary Hobbs flush on the jaw. Before he fell to the ground, Moody was on him, digging powerful fingers into the man's throat.

Gary, at the door, watched with horror. A flash pulled his eyes away to Morgan. Grinning, Morgan had his gun drawn and trained on the rolling gladiators, waiting for a clear shot.

Gary screamed. "No!" In an instant he climbed all over Morgan, almost jerking the man off balance in his fury. "No! You can't! Pop! Pop!"

On top of Hobbs now, the big man's back was a broad target. With a backward swipe of his hand, Morgan threw the boy off.

Gary landed hard against the wall of the shack as Morgan's gun spoke twice. The boy shivered as violently as if the slugs were tearing into his own small body. For a long moment he could not bring himself to turn, but lay sobbing and trembling, his face hidden in his arms.

The clatter of horses, receding in the distance, came through to him; then there was no sound but the frightened clucking of the chickens.

Gary turned slowly, already dreading to see what he knew he must find past the chicken coop. From behind the dung-whitened slats, the hand of Bill Moody, clutched in death, seemed to beckon. Gary raced the last few steps and threw himself with a wild cry on the humped, inert body that had been his father.

The men he passed on the splintered boardwalk under the shaded storefronts looked at Greg Farley in a new way now. Their eyes held more awe, their greetings were more deferential. Where he had been treated as an equal and

101

a friend before, he now was regarded as someone a little bigger than life, someone to hold a little bit in fear.

It was something to savor' something to learn to like. Only there wouldn't be time.

In two days at the most, the town's people would be filled with hate; and the open, welcoming hands would be white-knuckled around the stocks of rifles with nervous of steel on the triggers, determined to get Greg Farley, to make up for what he had done to their pride, their judgment of men, and their dignity. That would be the time to cringe, to avoid the sun again.

Jessica was at the teller's window, making change for a customer. "Twenty, twenty-five, thirty. That's correct, Mr. Henshaw?"

"Looks like that's all I'm goin' to get," the man said jovially. "Thank you, Miss Jessica."

He turned away. Jessica's pleasure at seeing Greg behind him was more than evident.

"Well! How are you, Mr. Farley?" Barker looked up from his desk; he rose and came forward. He greeted Greg effusively, for the obvious benefit of the watching customers.

But his eyes held a plea that belied the hearty words. "Business with the bank, Mr. Farley?" Greg looked at him coolly. There was nothing to gain by deflating this little man in his own bailiwick.

"Not hardly, Mr. Barker. My first pay ain't due for a while yet." Barker's gratitude was pathetic. "Yes, yes, of course. Now don't forget, we're always happy to serve you. How about that, Miss Jessica?"

Greg handed Jessica a slip of paper. "I just wanted to give you this receipt to take to your mother. It's from the feed store . . ."

Jessica took it. "Thank you. Mother told me you-"

"Mr. Farley! Mr. Farley!" Everyone in the bank turned to the breathless, tearstained boy who ran into Greg's arms and clung to him.

"What is it, Gary? What's the matter?" The feel of the trembling body in his arms was a trigger to memory. Larry had been like that once, small and dependent and needing comfort. The words came explosively, between sharp, painful gasps for air, hard to understand, yet terribly clear.

"Pop! They killed Pop!" Jessica was around the counter by that time, her skirts ballooning as she bent down to the boy. Her frightened glance met Greg's over the trembling head. She smothered Gary into her arms.

"You poor child!" Greg spoke gently, his face on a level with Gary's.

"Who was it, Gary? Who did it?" "The, man-that man with the scar . . ." Gary's finger traced a line from the curves of his mouth to the point of his dirt-streaked jaw. Greg looked across to Jessica.

"Morgan. He had a grudge against Bill Moody." Jessica said. "Can't you hurry out there? Maybe he's not-"

Greg straightened up to face Barker. "Get Doc Brown. I'll meet him hear."

Barker nodded, and Greg strode out of the bank. Doc Brown was there when he returned, his horse saddled, a rifle boot. A knot of people had collected about the almost hysterical boy. The doctor took a vial out of his bag.

"Give him some of this, Jessica. It'll quiet him." He looked at Greg. "I'm ready."

"Horses outside." Greg said quietly. "Come on."

Chapter 16

In the chicken-littered yard, Doc Brown examined the body. He indicated the two stains on the back of Moody's shirt. "Bears out the boy's story. Shot in the back while they were fighting."

Greg nodded and moved back to his horse. "Want me to come along?" Brown asked.

"That won't be necessary, Doctor. You'll be needed in town." He hesitated, then spoke steadily. "Take care of my prisoner." "Speaking of him-" Brown began. Greg turned to face him.

"Occur to you he might've been in on the Sedona bank robbery or the death of Marshal Fuller?" Greg kept his face a mask. "I aimed to question him, soon as he can talk."

"He's been talking already," Booth said. White lines showed around Greg's jaw. He waited.

"A word here and there. He kept muttering a name, too. Your name's Greg, isn't it?"

"Yes," said Greg, a split-second too late. Brown said, "I'm not asking any questions. I don't want Jessica hurt, Farley." He spoke with quiet intensity.

"I'm not a violent man, but if anyone hurt her-I could kill him without a twinge of regret." Greg, mounted, looked down without answering. Brown held his reins.

"Do we understand each other, Mr. Farley?" Their eyes met. "Reckon so, Doc."

Greg wheeled his mount and took off. Brown continued to squint after him in the sun until he rounded the corner of the unpainted shack and his shadow had disappeared from sight.

They came out of the coulee to a hump of ground. Hobbs twisted in the saddle. Watching him, Morgan spoke irritably.

"What you so spooked about, anyway?" "They'll be after us," Hobbs said. "You know they'll come after us."

"So what do you want me to do?" "You shouldn'ta killed him, Morgan. You didn't have no call to kill him. We was just rawhidin' him."

"Stow it, Morgan said irritably. "We was just rawhidin'." Hobbs seemed under a compulsion to relive the scene. "You coulda creased him with the barrel of your gun. That would've done it just as good."

"What I shoulda done I shoulda killed that kid." Morgan muttered under his breath. Hobbs twisted in his saddle again to look at the rolling mesquite hills behind them.

"I told you to stop it!" Morgan roared at him. Hobbs licked his dry lips. "I'm thinkin' about what that sheriff said. That mob-they'd just as soon string you up. An' he wouldn't stop 'em. Nor if it was you Morgan."

Morgan barked. "What do you mean-'you'? You're in this deep as me!" "I ain't the one that killed him," Hobbs said.

Morgan reined up and faced him. "What's on your mind, Hobbs?" Hobbs hesitated, sized up his man and took the risk of putting it into words.

"I think we oughta break up, Morgan." "You want out, is that it?" "Yeah, That's about it." Morgan eyed the greasy, frightened man contemptuously.

"Well, nobody's keepin' you." Hobbs eyes widened. This had been too easy. "You mean that, Morgan? No hard feelin's?"

"I wouldn't want to be saddled with you, you stinkin' yellow-belly." Morgan spat. "You want to get. So get!"

"Sure, Morgan. I-" Hobbs felt that something needed saying; some kind of a cap had to be put on the occasion. He couldn't think of one, not a good one.

"No hard feeling's," he began again, lamely. "So long, Morgan. Luck." Morgan did not answer as he watched Hobbs back receding into the coulee. He pulled his gun and shot twice.

Two small red holes appeared in the swat of the tight shirt. Hobbs sat upright in the stirrups for a moment, statue-like, then slowly tumbled off the horse and disappeared into the mesquite.

Morgan blew through the barrel of his gun. "No hard feelin's," he muttered. The trail was no problem to cut. Greg followed the clear marks of two horses over the hillocks of the valley. Only once did he have to dismount and study faint scratches on the hardpan before he picked up the direction.

From there it was a breeze, until he reached the spot where the two had separated. He rested a moment, shifting his saddle-weary rump, speculating; made up his mind, and followed the left fork.

A few minutes later, he saw the horse grazing in the coulee. Gun out, he proceeded cautiously. The roan reared dainty hooves to keep from stepping on Hobbs body, rolled under the mesquite brush.

Greg's thin lips tightened. He put up his gun, reined the roan about and headed for the other trail. It was as plain as a stage road, going higher and always higher into the wooded area that meant water.

And by running water, Greg found him. Morgan was drinking from cupped hands, while his horse watered below him in the creek, when Greg, dismounted, gun drawn, came noiselessly up behind him.

"All right, Morgan. On your feet." Morgan wheeled like lightning, six-gun flashing on the sun. Greg whipped his hand back across the hammer of his old single-action .44, and the slug spat between Morgan's feet.

"Don't give me an excuse to put the next one through your stinkin' gullet," Greg said Coldly. Morgan got to his feet slowly, shoving his gun back into the holster.

"You really *are* playin' sheriff, ain't you?" he said contemptuously. "Make a wrong move and find out," Greg said impassively. "You're making a mistake, Farley."

"You made the mistake, back at Bill Moody's place." Greg said. "Loosen that gun belt."

Morgan made no move to comply with the order. "What do they pay you for this, Farley? Fifty a month? Eighty?"

"The belt," said Greg laconically. "Forget that tin star, and I'll put you onto something good. Thousands." Hands on the belt buckle, Morgan, caught the flicker of interest in Greg's eye.

"And it's easy. A breeze'. My boss-my former boss-he's comin' in from Abilene with the cash from a thousand head of stock." "The belt," Greg repeated.

"He won't be lookin' for a heist, because he thinks he can't be picked up outside of town. But he can." Greg's eyes narrowed, and his nostrils flared, Morgan felt safer.

"And I'm the hombre that can do it. How' about it, Farley? You an' me! Forty grand if it's a dime, and all ours for the taking!" In spite of himself, Greg asked, "How do you figure to find him if no one else can?"

Morgan became cagey. "That's my insurance, Farley. Put up that gun, and I'll take you in." "Talk first," Greg ordered. "I can tell you one thing. You want to keep your eye on that filly of his. She's the marker."

Greg's expression changed, and his trigger finger whitened. Morgan whistled softly.

"So, that's the way the herd grazes! Say, you're something, all right! Only been in town three days and'-"

"Leave her out of it, Greg snapped. Morgan shrugged. "You're dealin'. See that valley? There's three passes-the north pass the south dip, an' that notch in the middle. The trick is to know which . . ."

In spite of himself, Greg's eyes flicked away from Morgan's to follow the other man's finger. This was the moment Morgan was waiting for. He went for the gun he had been too smart to drop. But the glint of iron caught the corner of Greg Farley's eye.

His .44 moved only inches, barked only once. A stunned, surprised look crossed Morgan's brows. He stood frozen in space, his gun only half out of its holster; disbelief washed over him like a heat wave, distorting his features as it passed. He looked down at the red stain already spreading over his gray shirt front.

The gun slipped out of his loose fingers, hung a moment by the trigger guard. Then dropped at his feet, a splash of his own blood on the barrel. A moment later, the spring went out of his knees, and he covered the gun with his body.

Greg watched him pitch forward and winced as the dead face smacked into the hardpan, as if taking the blow himself. Slowly the realization of what he had done came over Greg.

The gun in his hand began to shake. He looked down at it incredulously, as if accusing it of the monstrous act. The smooth stock and the metal barrel burned his hands; he flung the weapon back into its holster as if to get rid of something evil. He caught at a sapling to steady himself, his face contorted, tortured, and sick. Leaning over, he threw up. It didn't make him feel any better, for this was the first man that he ever killed.

Greg rode ahead at a walk, leading the two horse's, with the dead body's slung over their saddles. As they progressed down the street of Chino Wells, loafers straightened their chairs in front of the general store, heads popped out of windows, men and women stopped on the boardwalk to watch silently.

Greg looked neither to right or left; he ignored the populace as if they did not exist. Under the shade of the broad-brimmed sombrero, the tense, stricken lines were still to be seen etched in his face'.

He turned in at the shop of J. C. Lesko, the undertaker, and looped his bridle over the hitching post. Lesko, in his black rubber apron, came out of the shop with two little hand carts. The two men did not speak as they dumped the two body's on to the carts and unceremoniously trundled them into the shop.

Greg watched as the two disappeared, then remounted and headed down the street. Little knots of people gathered, whispering together, waiting to see where Greg went next. He dismounted at Dr. Brown's office.

Larry was lying in semi-darkness on the Doctor's leather-covered couch. He was still as Greg entered the door, then thrashed about aimlessly and began to mutter. Only a few words came through, only half-understood.

"Greg shouldn't do it for me. Always been good at getting' li'l brother outa scrapes . . ." A slight movement on the other side of the darkened surgery flipped Greg's eyes away from the wounded boy. He made out Jessica, sitting in an armchair with a sleeping Gary cradled in her arms. Gary's teary-wet cheek was against the sprigged dimity of her bosom. Her eyes smoldered at Greg in disbelieving surmise. The inner door opened, and Brown was framed in its light.

Larry turned again, his voice more insistent now. "Watch it! Here, here, Greg; I got the money! Get him! He's got my gun . . ."

He subsided, his utterances trailing away into unintelligible dribbled syllables. For a moment the three adults made a motionless tableau, only their eyes talking. Speech was torn out of Jessica first.

Jim told me, but I didn't want to believe him." Jessica's unconscious tensing woke the boy in her arms. He spied Greg and leaped to his feet.

"Did you get Them, Mr. Farley? Did you get the dirty rats that killed my Pop?" "Yes, Gary. I got them." "You killed them, didn't you, Mr. Farley? You gunned them down, just like they gunned down Pop?"

Greg swallowed cotton as the scene passed before his mind's eye. "There dead, Gary."

"I'm glad! Thank you, Mr. Farley! You gave those dirty skunks what was comin' to them!"

"There, there, Gary!" Jessica tried to quiet the overwrought boy. "Mustn't get yourself worked up, old-timer," Brown said. Greg nodded; unable to speak to the boy, he tousled the untidy hair. He tried to make the gesture as he pointed over his shoulder to Larry.

"All right to move him?" he asked Brown. "Where to?" Greg's face and voice were flat.

"Jail. That's where he belongs." Brown paused. "I reckon so."

Jessica started. "Jim!"

Brown silenced her with a look. Greg pretended not to hear the shocked syllable, but went to the black leather couch. Brown came over to help him.

"Get on his good side," Brown said. Greg took Larry's good arm, looped it about his own neck, and lifted the unconscious man to his feet. Larry groaned

Greg roughened his voice. "All right, fella. Got a nice warm cell ready for you!"

112

Jessica looked on, horrified. But Gary forgot his own troubles in his lively interest in the new diversion.

"Gosh, Mr. Farley, what'd he do?"

"That's what I aim to find out, soon's he can talk."

"Li'l brother! Always getting' in jams," Larry muttered groggily. "Shut up!" Greg said through his teeth. As soon as Brown closed the door behind them, Jessica leaped on him like a tigress.

"That man is in no condition-Jim, how could you?" Brown put both hands on her shoulders. "Shh, Jessica! Don't mix in! You wouldn't believe me before. Now you've seen and heard for yourself." His voice was compassionate, sincere.

"I'm only trying to spare you pain, Jessica darling. You don't know this man Farley."

She snapped angrily, "I know all I need!"

"He rode in from nowhere. I don't care about his past; I don't care what he does from here on. But he's not for you! Sure, I'd resent any man who looked at you. I'm in love with you. But this time I'm right. Stay away from him! You can't trust that man!"

Jessica flashed out angrily, "I'll decide who to trust!" A sidewise glance from Brown stopped her in mid-sentence.

She followed his eyes to Gary's, small in the big chair, his own grief forgotten as he listened with open mouth and wide eyes to the quarreling pair.

Chapter 17

Larry snored gently on the pallet in the cell as Greg came over to him, bent down and shook him gently. "Larry. Gotta get up, Larry."

Larry opened his eyes, took in his surrounding, and felt quick fear at the sight of bars.

"It's all right, Larry. I'm the sheriff, remember?" Greg lifted the younger man's shoulders. "Come on, kid. I let you rest as long as I could. We gotta make tracks."

Larry got to a sitting position with Greg's help, gasping violently and clapping a hand to his wound. "All right, Larry?" Larry nodded.

"I'll help you with your horse. I took 'em off before." Larry looked at Greg's back over the boots. "The job, Greg." "We're skipping it." "Money-" "We'll make out." Larry yanked his foot out of Greg's hands.

"We need that money!" Bootless, he staggered to his feet and out of the cell. Greg stared after him! "Larry!"

Larry reached the gun rack on the wall and snatched down a rifle. Leaning against the rack to maintain his balance, breathing hard and shallowly, he turned the gun on the startled Greg. There was no mistaking his deadly seriousness.

Greg held himself rigid and kept his voice down. "Put that rifle down, Larry."

"Oh, no. *I'll* call the shots, big brother. Big hero! Always got everything under control!" Greg took a step toward him, then halted at the ominous click of the hammer.

"You're wondering if I'd really do it, if I'd really kill big-brother Greg, who wet-nursed me up from a runt dogie. Get between me an' that money an' find out!" He waited, but Greg was motionless. "You're smart, Greg. I always gave you credit for that. You know I'd shoot, don't you? You couldn't if it was the other way around, but I can. And by God, I will, It-"

He took a vicious delight in needling Greg. "That badge is blinding you, isn't it? Forgetting why you put it on? Let me remind you. To pull a job! To make a haul! Now you want to keep it? Be a real sheriff? Not in the cards, brother."

He jerked his head toward the window. "Look out there. That's a telegraph office. How long will it take to get a man here from Sedona to take a look at you?" He shoved the muzzle of the rifle into Greg's stomach. "I'll tell you what you're going to do!"

Greg ignored the bite of the steel; his eyes took on a faraway look. "You're right, Larry. I've been a fool to think-things have been happening to me these last few days. It's been kind of like looking in a window. You don't realize how cold and miserable you are till you see the folks inside, warm and comfortable and happy an' safe. I kind of hoped there might be a place inside for us . . ."

Larry gauged his brother's mood and took instant, cunning advantage of it. "We could do it, Greg! If we got away from here, somewhere else-"

"Yeah." Greg breathed new hope. Larry felt him out. "We'll need a stake." "No!" Greg shouted explosively.

"Miller an' Gorman won't let us go easy." He saw Greg's hesitation, and pushed harder.

"But if they got their cut, just this once-" His voice trembled with eagerness. "We'll need 'em anyway. Then we'll pull loose. The last job, Greg!.

The sound of horses' hooves approaching cut Greg's reply short. "Quick back in the cell."

He helped Larry back to the pallet and pulled the blanket over him. Turning, he saw the tight-bodied, full-skirted silhouette of Jessica Brice in the street doorway.

He came forward, his surprise showing. "Jessica-" The tremor of a frightened bird shook her, unbidden, as the big man towered over her. She had come in one impulse, and now she questioned her instinct.

"I'm taking Gary home with me." "That's good. He shouldn't have to go back there." She looked toward the cell. Greg said, "Jessica, I have to tell you-" She interrupted, "Please, Greg. You don't owe me any explanation."

"As soon as I can move him, I'm taking him away." "But you mustn't!" It came out impulsively; then, catching herself, "Chino Wells needs you." Greg shook his head.

"That's not true, Greg! Whatever happened in the past, stays in the past. Nobody cares. It's what they see in you now. Ask anybody!" "Anybody?" he asked softly.

"You should hear what Mr. Barker says, and Mayor Gifford . . ." "And you?"

"I'll show you how I feel." She hesitated, then plunged ahead. "I'm riding out tomorrow to meet my father. I want you to come with me."

"Larry, listening on the pallet, tensed. "Every year at trail time, Dad tells me which pass he'll come in on. It's our little secret." Jessica stopped herself. Perhaps she regretted her impulse.

"Those men from Sedona are still at large. I'd feel safer with you." Greg said, "What if those men are closer than you think?" Determined, Jessica insisted, "I'd still feel safer-with you, Meet me at-" He stopped her lips. "No, Jessica. Don't say it." He kept his fingers on her face, running the tips over her cheek, reluctant to lose the contact. Her eyes lifted to his, and her mouth tilted. He bent down and kissed her, tenderly, reverently.

After he released her, she looked up at him for a sign of relenting; then she turned and ran out of the door. Greg looked after her as she climbed into the trap beside the bundled from of Gary and slapped the horse's rump with the reins. He turned to face a snarling Larry. "You had that little filly eatin' out of your hand! An' you let her go! She was goin' to tell you, an' you stopped her!"

"That's right. Look, if you're strong enough to move around, we'll get goin'." Greg made a move to go past Larry; but the younger man caught him by the shoulder and whirled him around to face the window. "Goin'," Larry snarled caustically. "Take a look!"

Greg looked. Across the street a man was knocking at the door of the darkened telegraph office. He was only a shadow and unidentifiable, until the light went on in the office and revealed the form of Dr. Jim Brown. The telegrapher spoke with him a moment on the stoop, then admitted him and shut the door.

"What'd I tell you?" Larry demanded. "They'll be after us now, fast," Greg said, half to himself. Larry talked into his ear. "There's one thing faster, Greg! *Money!* Forty thousand dollars will buy fresh horses! Men will forget they saw us for the kind of money we can show 'em!"

He had Greg going-he could see that. He talked faster, more urgently. "We been through the other thing: winded nags, no grub, and every man's hand against us! It's that or steal! You gotta kill a man to take his horse!"

"No!" "The last job, Greg! I want to try that before I go straight. You make it sound good. Give me a chance!"

Greg paused a long moment, searching Larry's face, probing his sincerity. At last he spoke.

"Let's get one thing straight, Larry. No gunplay." Larry was elated, ready to promise the moon.

"No gunplay." He agreed fervently.

"We've never lied to each other, kid."

"I mean it, Greg. I swear it."

"We can get that money peaceable. I want your solemn word."

Larry looked him straight in the eye.

"You've got it."

Steven E. Farley

Chapter 18

The sun was rising in a cloudless copper sky. It would be hot today, thought Jessica, riding the gray gelding toward the white arch of the Lazy *S*. Dad liked her in a blue shirt and jeans: it partially made up to him for the lack of the boy he'd wanted. She forced a thousand inconsequential thoughts through her mind to keep out of the one thing she dared not admit. She came to the gate, stopped in its long shadow and looked toward town.

The road, as far as she could see to the turn, was empty of life. Jessica pursed her lips and bit off her disappointment. He wasn't coming. Her face lit up at the puff of dust that rose beyond the hillock. She waited, ashamedly realizing her heart was speeding its best, that the perspiration forming on her palms under the riding gloves was not from the fresh born sun. She held back as long as she could, then spurred the gelding to met Greg.

He was grave and somewhat embarrassed. "Jessica, I-" She gestured to stop him.

"Please. You don't have to say anything." She could see the gratitude of a man not at home with words, or so she thought. She did not see the shame he felt at being there under false colors. To mask his feeling, he made a move to start up. Jessica put a hand on his arm to stop him.

"Wait." She gestured with her head. "We've got company." Greg followed her look. A piebald pony kicked dust along the trail from the ranch house. With a start Greg identified the pony's rider.

"Gary?" He turned to Jessica. "You're taking him along?" "It'll take his mind off his troubles." Gary called out delightedly, "Mr. Farley! Miss Jessica didn't tell me you was comin' along!"

"I wasn't sure myself until just now, Gary." Jessica smiled. Greg was troubled. "Do you think-I mean, after all, this is no pleasure trip . . ."

Gary crowed cheerfully. "let 'em try to rob us! We'll give it to 'em won't we, Mr. Farley?" He drew a pair of imaginary guns. "Bang! Bang! Giddap! After 'em!"

He dug his heels into the pony and galloped ahead of them down the road. Jessica looked after him. "Wonderful how he bounces back, isn't it?" She turned to Greg. "A boy needs a hero, and I've got a feeling you're elected."

Greg did not return her smile, but dug spurs into the roan's flank. Her brow puzzled, Jessica followed.

The sun tipped over the false fronts of Chino Wells when Dr. Brown left the office that was home to him and walked the hundred yards to the Sheriff's office. He met few townspeople so early in the morning, for which he was grateful. Never a talkative man, Brown found it hard to maintain the small amenities that made for success where the afflicted could come to him or do with out.

When the Doctor was poor, too many chose the latter course. Brown had spent a restless night after Jessica left him so angrily. He had the natural repulsion of an honest man against turning informer, but a man had been killed, a lawman whom Brown had known and liked. He was reasonably sure the wounded boy was connected with that crime; and that the new sheriff of Chino Wells was more than casually connected with the boy.

In telegraphing to Sedona he found out that a Deputy U. S. Marshal had left for Chino Wells two-day's ago using the Abilene trail. He had only done his duty. Duty-not jealousy-had prompted him, he told himself sharply. But he could not believe his own assurance.

He dismounted, turned into the open door of the sheriff's office, with words half uttered.

"Thought I'd look in on the patient . . . " His voice trailed off as he realized he was talking to empty air. He stared at the open cell door, turned and saw no horses beside his own sorrel at the rail outside.

All right. Farley had taken the hint, gotten out of town with his brother. Brown stood in the empty, dusty office, savoring the relief that washed over him. He was glad to get Greg Farley out of his hair. He'd rather see it this way than the other-when the U.S Marshal from Sedona arrived.

Greg Farley was a rival-a criminal, perhaps; yet Dr. Jim Brown wished him luck. A brave man deserved no less. Dr. Brown mounted his horse to finish his morning rounds.

The sun was halfway to its zenith as the three men on the knife-ridge sat overlooking the valley. Mounted, they let their horses' heads down to graze on the inhospitable dry scrub as they squinted into the heat-shimmering bowl below them.

Ben miller wiped his neck with a bandana and squinted into the sun. "We been here more'n an hour. He could be givin' us the go-by."

"Not Greg," Larry said confidently. "He'll show." "A man'll do funny things where a woman's concerned," Gorman opined. "I told you not to worry," Larry said. We coulda grabbed that girl. Give me five minutes, I'd know which way to look," Miller said grimly.

"Maybe you would and maybe you wouldn't." Miller permitted himself a lewd grin.

"Well, I'd sure have fun trying'." Larry broke open the breech of his rifle and checked the load. Gorman looked on anxiously.

"Didn't you promise Greg there'd be no shootin?" Larry grinned. "Sure, I promised." Gorman chuckled. "Greg ain't gonna like it." "He'll come around. Right now he's got that girl on the brain. When he gets over it, he'll agree my way is better." He slapped the rifle significantly. "When there's no witnesses, there's no conviction. It's always been a good rule and still is."

The sun was close to announcing noon as Dr. Brown carefully flexed the swollen and twisted knuckles on Wong's right hand. The rheumatism was getting worse, no doubt about it. The hand would soon be useless. "Wong, you old heathen, how old are you?"

"Wong grinned toothily. "*Yessee! Yessee!*" Mrs. Brice, hovering over them, clucked and shook her head. "I declare, he wouldn't tell you if he could talk civilized. But he's seventy if he's a day. Been with us nigh onto twenty years, and he looked just the same then as he does now!"

Brown stood up. "Well, not much I can do for him, I'm afraid. Continue the hot soaking." He tried to keep his voice casual. "Didn't pass Jessica on the way out. Did she go to the bank today?" "Why, no, Jim, didn't she till you? She went to meet her father. Took Gary with her." She walked to the front door with Brown.

"Got herself all slicked up like she was meeting a beau, she did. I twitted her about it: never saw her touch up her face just to meet her old pa!" She stopped at the door.

"Thanks for coming, Jim. I'll see that Wong soaks that hand, you can depend on it." The door closed on her chatter, and Brown thoughtfully headed for his horse. Strange ideas ran through his head, fearless ideas. Jessica was a headstrong girl, but she wouldn't.

He had to make sure, He swung to the saddle, but instead of turning the horse's head back to town, where patients waited, he pulled the rein and started toward the rim of the valley where the three notches marked the three possible trails in from Abilene.

The Morning heat was piling up. Larry lay in the shade, panting, fighting pain in the side, while Miller wiped sweat out of his eyes and scanned the baking valley. "What time you make it?" Gorman asked petulantly. "Hour till," Miller said. Gorman peered over the valley. "Empty as a church," he pronounced. "I say they ain't comin'." Miller grinned back at Larry, "Well, you better get your eyes fixed up, old man!"

The others followed Miller's pointing finger and picked out the specks far below, visible only by the dust they raised, coming in from the town pass to the south. For the time being, it was impossible to tell which of the three passes they were heading for, as they turned first toward one, then toward another, threading through the boulders and finding the easiest trail. Gorman said, "Wonder why Greg don't give us some sign." Larry grunted. "Probably don't know himself yet. But it won't be hard to tell, once they make their move." Unseen by the three men, and not seeing them in turn, another watcher waited for the indication that would show him how to cut off the group in the valley.

When it came, it came suddenly. One moment the trail of the group in the valley was aimless and wandering; the next, it trended unmistakably in the direction of the north notch. Larry, Gorman and Miller exchanged simultaneous elated looks. They mounted, wheeled, and raced down the backside of the hogback.

Brown caught the message at the same instant. He too wheeled and headed for the north pass. In the valley, Greg fell behind the others. His eyes went up to the ridge. He knew there was nothing to see, but his mind ground out the picture as clearly as if it were in front of him.

"Coming, Mr. Farley?" Greg kneed the roan. "Coming, Gary." The two galloped to catch Jessica, already going out of sight up ahead.

Chapter 19

The country beyond the north notch was open and rolling. As it spread out in front of him, Greg glanced at the sides of the pass. They were craggy and rock-strewn, ideal for ambush.

A cry from Jessica brought his eyes forward. He saw the three riders then, coming toward the fork from the north. Jessica gave rein to her gelding, his hooves thundering to meet the newcomers.

Brice rode a little ahead of his two Men. He was beefy and solid, with small red veins crisscrossing his tanned cheeks; yet there was enough resemblance for Greg to recognize Jessica's father, even if he hadn't seen her throw her arms about him as they met.

"Daddy! It's so good to see you!"

"Hi, baby. You're a sight for sore eyes," Brice had boomed out affectionately.

"Daddy, this is Mr. Farley, our new sheriff." Brice had looked Greg up and down with keen gray eyes. "Well, things happen when the old man goes away! Pleased to meet you,

Mr. Farley." "You know Gary Moody, Dad. So you see I have plenty of protection."

"Hi, Gary. You're Bill Moody's boy, ain't you?" Jessica had headed him off quickly. "I'll talk to you about that later, Dad." She turned to Greg. "Mr. Fraley, meet Archie Ryan and Jake Franco."

"Howdy," Greg acknowledged the introduction. The two trail hands nodded. They regarded him coolly, rifles casual but ready; to them the badge was not a voucher for the man behind it.

"So we got a sheriff, eh?" Aaron Brice said. "About time, I'd say."

Greg deprecated, "Just temporary, Mr. Brice, till the next election." Jessica said quickly, pride sounding in her voice, "Mayor Bailey and Mr. Barker aren't worried about that. And when you hear the way Greg-I mean Mr. Farley-has been performing, neither will you."

"Brice hugged her. "Well, that's good enough for me. Say, why are we frizzling out here in the heat? I'm hankering' for a good home-cooked meal, an' so are the boys. Ain't had fittin' grub since we left home!"

Jessica laughed. "Don't give me that! You know you painted Abilene red!" Jake spoke up. "Well, maybe a mite pink, Miss Jessica."

Brice rode ahead with Jessica. "How's Mom, baby?" Jessica's answer was lost in the noise of hooves. Gary grinned at Greg. "Come on, Mr. Farley." Greg nodded, and Gary spurred the pinto ahead. Greg waited for Archie and Jake to go on, but the two trail hands held back.

"Lead the way, Sheriff," said Archie, unsmiling. Jake waved him ahead with his rifle. Greg noted he hadn't restored it to its boot. He felt a twinge of concern. These men were not going to be easy.

"They re-entered the pass. Greg furtively scanned the rock walls. Archie and Jake, ever watchful, altered their strategy according to what was evidently a pre-conceived plan. Leaving Jake to bring up the rear, Archie spurred ahead, passed Greg, Jessica, Brice, and Gary, and went out of sight around the turn up forward.

He was waiting for them when they drew up. Only then did he continue around the next gooseneck in the trail.

Behind the high rocks, Larry heard the first hoof beat's. He frowned warningly at Miller and Gorman. They nodded back. Wearied from the hard ride, Larry lay on the grass; he pulled his rifle to him and steadied it on a rock.

Down below they could see the party approach. But before the victims were close enough to challenge, a puzzled look crossed Larry's brow. His quick ears caught sounds from another direction. He rose and strained for a look.

Jim Brown was galloping into the pass from the south. "The devil!" cried Gorman.

"He's gonna meet 'em!" Larry's teeth ground together. "No, he won't." His rifle came up, and he sighted down at the approaching rider. Ben Miller angrily knocked the barrel of the weapon up.

"You darn fool!" Larry subsided, saying nothing. The three waited for developments. Archie had his rifle ready before Doc. Brown appeared around the rock wall. But he recognized the doctor, and lowered the rifle with a puzzled look.

Jessica, too, was surprised. "Jim!" Brown ignored her and pointed at Greg accusingly.

"This man-he's up to no good!" Brice creased his betting brows. "He's the sheriff!" Greg tensed in the saddle. Without even looking, he could sense Archie and Jake behind him, their muzzles lifted to his back.

Brown pressed on. "Nobody in Chino Wells saw him till three days ago. His brother is an outlaw; shot in a robbery over at Sedona. Now his brother is missing from the jail. He's pulling something, I tell you!"

From the height, Larry pulled himself forward. He couldn't make out the words, but the tension in the group below was unmistakable. "Greg's in trouble." He aimed his rifle and fired a shot. The bullet kicked up dust between Greg and Brown, causing the horses to shy.

Archie and Jake reined about to look upward. Instantly Greg had his gun out.

"All right, folks. Drop your guns."

Chapter 20

The two trail hands whipped back and found themselves looking down Greg's gun muzzle. The ugly lead glint of the .44 could be seen in the holes of the cylinder.

They looked up. Three figures stood, straddle-legged against the sky, rifles trained on the group below. Taken by complete surprise, the victims froze tight. Only Gary moved, coming closer to Jessica. She put a protective arm about him, not seeing him, her face sculptured into marble cameo of horror and disbelief.

"Greg waved the six-shooter. "Your guns." Reluctantly, Archie and Jake dropped their rifles and side arms. Their horses shied at the metallic clatter on the rocks at their feet. Only Brice still remained unmoving.

Jake said quietly, "Better do what he says, Mr. Brice. They got us cold." Brice released the buckle of his gun belt and let it slide down the flanks of his horse to the ground. Greg had to pass Jessica and Gary to get to Brice. He did not try to lift his eyes as he passed. His voice was unnecessarily harsh. "Down, everybody. Off your mounts."

They obeyed silently. Greg felt their hate and contempt, like a solid wall. His lips clamped tight; he kicked the guns out of reach as he moved to Brice's horse and opened the stuffed saddlebags.

"How about it, Greg?" Larry called from the ridge. Not trusting himself to speak, Greg waved an okay signal, detached the saddlebags and slung them to his horse….

Greg rode back, slapping the other horses with his quirt; they snorted and skittered away. He found himself facing Gary's tragic disillusion. Greg felt the self-imposed defense of silence breaking down before the boy's bitter accusation. "Gary-"

Gary's rock-hard expression did not change. Greg made an ineffectual gesture toward the rifles on the ridge. "Gary, he's my brother…We got to make it to the border before the law catch the both of us….He's hurt, Gary…."

It was no use, of course. He turned to Jessica, and again the floodgates of speech broke down. "Jessica, that's why we need the money. The only reason." He was talking to stone.

"Hey, Farley, get on with it!" Miller growled from the ridge. Greg turned his roan and headed up the slop to join the others. He could feel eyes boring and burning into his back as he went.

He saw the fire spurt from Larry's rifle and stared at it for a split-second, not believing the blast that roared past his ears. He turned his head. Larry was clutching his midsection. He groaned and fell into the dust. "Larry!" Out of the corner of his eye Greg saw Jake make a run for the rifle, ten paces away from him on the ground. Larry's rifle spoke once more, and Jake crumpled, his out-stretched fingers inches from the Winchester.

"Larry!" Greg screamed. "Stop!"

"Too late, Greg! Can't leave witnesses now!" Over his shoulder, Greg called, "Make for cover. Quick!"

He wheeled his mount to ride between Jessica and Gary and the murderously accurate fire from Larry's weapon. Larry first thought the interposition was accidental. "Greg!" he called out, holding his fire impatiently. "Get outa the way!"

It was Gorman who first divined Greg's purpose. "He's coverin' 'em!"

"I'll stop that," Larry muttered. He fired; Greg's roan stumbled and fell. Greg managed to leap clear. Larry pumped quick shots across his brother's body. The slugs kicked up dust too close for comfort as Jessica grabbed Gary around the cover of rocks.

"Larry!" Greg called again, with all the authority he could muster. "Hold Fire!"

Larry laughed shortly. "I'm calling the shots, big brother!" Lying in the dirt, Greg aimed his six-shooter up the hill, but did not fire.

Gary stared, wide-eyed. "Mr. Farley-which side is he on?" "I wonder if he knows," Jessica murmured, half to herself. "But why don't he shoot?" Brice shook his head.

"That rifle got him out ranged." Greg, standing in the clearing, looked at the nearest Winchester, it was Archie's, estimating his chances of reaching it.

"Don't try it, brother," Larry warned. Despite the warning, Greg made a dash for the rifle. Larry was taken by surprise. Breathing hard from the excitement and exertion, he wasted seconds training his gun and firing. Even so, the bullet was faster than the man.

Larry's slug spat dust between Greg and his goal. Instinctively Greg pulled back, his spurs digging tracks in the dirt at his sudden stop. Unable to employ their shorter-range hand guns, Gorman and Miller could only watch and await for developments.

Larry shouted, "I can do better any time, big brother. You know that." Greg, behind the cover of a big rock, knew it only too well. The rifle lay tantalizingly near, just beyond three feet of deadly sunlight.

Miller surreptitiously signaled Gorman to stay put, turned and slid through the brush, crouching low. Larry strained to see what Greg was up to behind the rock. All he could see were the rifles. Then, oddly, a black line snaked out to the nearest weapon. Puzzled, he looked again.

Greg pulled in the gun belt and tried again. It was no easy trick, trying to catch the hammer or trigger guard with the buckle. Larry watched the slight movement of the brush as Ben Miller bellied around, out of sight. He grinned to himself, and on Greg's second try with the belt, he fired. The slug tore into the stock of the Winchester, jerking it away from the searching belt buckle.

Greg pulled the gun belt back, and leaned against the rock to steady himself for his next attempt. Moments passed. Larry lay with his rifle barrel notched and ready, but the waiting told on his already jangled nerves. He muttered between clenched teeth.

"Go on. Why don't you make your play?" Greg made it. He flipped the belt. Gorman, watching the contest tensely, could not refrain from calling out, "There he goes!"

Miraculously, his belt buckle caught on the rifle's hammer. But the end of the belt was now out where Greg would have to expose his arm to reach it. Again he waited, let the tension build up in the dry, dust-choked battleground.

He picked up a rock and shied it to one side, where it rustled and hissed through brush before striking ground again. Simultaneously he reached for the belt. And simultaneously, Larry's rifle rang out, reverberating through the still valley. "Ha!" Larry saw with satisfaction the red stain spread over Greg's arm. "Didn't expect me to fall for that one, did you, big brother?" Greg winced and set his teeth against the pain. His fingers clutched the near end of the belt; he did not dare release them and lose his precarious hold. He forced himself to draw on the belt, very gently and very slowly.

It was a ticklish job. Larry fired again; and this time Greg cried out as the pain seared his forearm. But he had been expecting the pain. Sheer nerve kept his arm steady; the rifle rasped over the rocks, ever closer to his reach.

Now at last his hand was back under cover, safe from Larry's slugs. But Larry had sent one into the stock of the Winchester. It jumped from the ground, dislodging the buckle.

Gary gasped. Jessica, white-faced, held him tightly as she watched. Gary's sharp ears caught the sound of rustling in the brush; his head turned. "Sheriff, look out, behind you!"

The brush rustled again, and Miller stood up from behind it, his six-gun trained on Greg. A rifle shot rang out from a different direction, as Miller grunted as the lead plowed into his body. He fired once, wildly; then his eyes closed as he sank down out of sight into the brush.

Groman's mouth dropped open as he watched his friend fall. Suddenly panicked, he stood up as a rifle bullet from below cut into his mid-section killing him, as his body slid down the slope until the brush stopped him.

Larry's eyes were jerked away from Greg as Greg reached for the rifle. Larry was looking for who ever fired those two shots with such accuracy, from long distances.

Larry could see a man running up to the four behind the rock, keeping low as he went.

Jessica, looking him over as he ran up to them, noticing the Badge on his vest. Doc Brown also saw the badge, saying. "Thank you for your help! Are you the Man form Sedona?" Brown asked.

Stan looked at Doc in puzzlement? "Yes sir, I'm Stan Rhodes, Deputy U.S. Marshal. But how did you now?"

"I'm Dr. Brown. I sent a telegram to Sedona, that the four men that robbed your bank and killed the banker are here in Chino Wells, and the Sheriff there, said that you were on your way, when the town found out that Marshal Fuller had been killed. And that man you just killed is part of the gang." Stan asking doc. "And the other Three?" Doc looking at Jessica and back at the Marshal.

"The one behind the rock, his name is Greg Farley and the one on top of the slope, is his brother Larry, and the other man you shot.

Jessica spoke up "And Greg is also Sheriff, of Chino Wells. If it wasn't for him we would all be dead!"

Stan looked at Jessica. "Sheriff?"

"It's a long story Marshal. We'll explain it to you later!" Stan yelled out from behind the rock. "Greg Farley,

136

you all right?" Greg saw the badge on the vest of the young lawman as he came running down the trail, under the circumstance, he was glad to see him! "My right arm is a little shot up." Greg said in pain.

"You, Larry Farley, This is Deputy U.S. Marshal Stan Rhodes, come on down. This is the end of the trail for you!"

A shot from Larry's rifle spattered rock splinters over the partially exposed Marshal. Greg yelled back to the lawman. "Stay behind the rock Marshal, he's very good with that rifle." Greg turning over on the ground saw the saddlebags and looked to see if he could see Brice and tossed them to him.

"I won't be needing that, Mr. Brice. One way or the other." He made a vague gesture toward the still forms of Archie and Jake. "I'm sorry," he began. Then his words died of their own inadequacy. He leaned against the rock to catch his breath before he was able to project his voice. "Larry!"

There was no answer from the slope. "Larry! I'm coming after you!" Larry's mouth twisted in savage satisfaction. "By God, big brother, you do that!"

Winding a bandana about his bleeding arm, Greg paused at the vicious tone.

"Stinkin' lawmen! By God, Miller was right. He said you was nothin' but a stinkin' lawman in your heart! I shoulda knowed it before-when you let Marshal Fuller ride us into the ground an' never raised a finger!" Greg closed his eyes a minute, then knotted the bandana with his teeth.

Larry's voice screamed at him, piercing into his ears. "But you'd gun down your own brother fast enough! *He's* on the outside! That makes everything just fine!"

Greg hefted the Winchester into his good arm. Larry's voice bore down on him again.

"All right, you yellowbellied lawman; Come an' get me-if you got the guts!" Larry rolled about quickly, finding a better spot. When Greg stepped out into the open, Larry was completely hidden from sight.

Slowly Greg started across the clearing. Three steps-five-ten-and still no action from the slope. Rifle aimed and ready, Greg watched for the slightest movement.

When it came, it was sudden: a spurt of fire from the least likely manzanita. The slug caught Greg below the knee. He clutched his leg and sprawled in the dust. But his eyes did not blink for an instant. He knew Larry's location now; the sun glinting on the younger man's gun barrel was merely verification. Lying on his side, Greg fired at the flash. He waited, a sitting duck if he had missed.

The last reverberations faded into the mountains of silence; and Greg knew he had not missed. There was no elation in him. Slow, painfully, using the rifle as a crutch, he worked his way to his feet.

Greg toiled up the slope on sheer grit. His face was agonized, not alone by his physical suffering. Each step was a new torture, so that it seemed impossible to take the next; yet somehow the next step was taken-until he heard a groan beneath his feet and there were no more steps to take.

Larry was lying face down. Greg turned him over, wiping the sweat and dust from his face. The boy managed the ghost of a smile, a ghost that winged through Greg's heart as he saw it on the other Larry, the boy of six. There was admiration in it, and respect of a kind.

"Shouldn'ta tried to take you on, big brother. Not after you got hold of *that* rifle. You always had it over me, when things was even."

"Don't talk, Larry." Greg heard the running footsteps behind him. "The Doc's here."

"He can't do nothing' for me. Not any more." "Don't say that, kid." Greg's voice changed. A vicious note came to the fore.

"You always come out on top, don't you, big brother?" Larry shifted in Greg's arms.

"I couldn't rest easy if you came out on top this time-this last-" His gun hand came out from under cover of his body. He had his .44 revolver in it, already drawn, and cocked, waiting for this moment and fired.

The bullet hit Greg in the chest, above his heart. Greg, still holding Larry in his arm's eased the limp body gently to the ground, saying brokenly, "I never knew, kid. I never knew." Brown was behind him then. He bent down, gently removed Greg, and bent down to Larry, lifting one eyelid. A single glance at the glazed eye told him all he needed to know. He caught Greg's pained, questioning look, shook his head, and gruffly turned his attention to Greg's own wounds. Greg muttered brokenly. "I never knew he hated me, so!"

It was Jessica's voice that answered him. "He didn't, really. It was his need of you. That's what he hated." He looked up at her, desperately wanting to believe her. Jessica nodded.

"He needn't have been ashamed. We all need someone."

A shadow fell over Greg. He looked up; it was the young lawman. The Marshal, looking down at Greg as the Doc worked on him. "Is, he going to be ok, Doc?" Doc Brown, looked up at the young marshal and shook his head, as the blood-stain spread from his shirt to the badge on his chest.

"Gary, where's Gary?" Greg asked. "I'm here, Mr. Farley!" as the young boy kneeled down beside him. "Gary, I'm sorry about, all that's happened to you. And getting you all caught up in this; Please forgive me!" Gary with tears, running down his face. "Sheriff, Please don't, Die!" "Doc, look after 'em, bot--" Greg fell limp. Doc looked at him and looked back at the girl. "He's dead, Jessica." She and Gary held each other as the Marshal reached down to take the badge from Greg's shirt. "No, leave it! He earned it!" Jessica said.

Doc nodded, as his hand sought Jessica's, as he tousled Gary's hair with the other, and walked down the slope.

*****

About The Author

See, Steven E. Farley's two other great book's - About the Author-. "Child of the Lion" and "The Mormon Mountain Meadows Massacre" by 1stbooks Library.

Printed in the United States
33606LVS00001B/196-204

9 781418 422066